CONTENTS

2/98

KEYS TO SINGLE PARENTING

Carl E. Pickhardt, Ph.D.

BARRON'S

Cover photo © Ron Chapple/FPG International Corp

DEDICATION
To my wife, Irene, who provided much appreciated editorial help during the final stages of this manuscript, and to the Barbara Bauer Literary Agency, who found a home for this book.

The material in this book is drawn from three sources: ten years of writing columns for *The Single Parent Magazine*; conducting numerous parenting workshops; and counseling many single parents in my private practice as a psychologist. All examples and quotes given, however, are fictitious inventions created to illustrate a psychological point

All inquiries should be addressed to·
Barron's Educational Series, Inc.
250 Wireless Boulevard
Hauppauge, New York 11788

Library of Congress Catalog Card No.: 95-20820

International Standard Book No. 0-8120-9331-3

Library of Congress Cataloging-in-Publication Data
Pickhardt, C. E. (Carl E.), 1939–.
    Keys to single parenting / C. E. Pickhardt.
      p. cm. — (Barron's parenting keys)
    Includes bibliographical references and index.
    ISBN 0-8120-9331-3 (pbk.)
    1. Single parents. 2. Single-parent family. 3. Parenting.
I. Title. II. Series.
HQ759.915.P53   1996
306.85′6—dc20   95-20820
                                      CIP

PRINTED IN THE UNITED STATES OF AMERICA
6789   9770   987654321

Part Ten—The Abandoned Single Parent

INTRODUCTION

A ccording to the 1990 U.S. census, 30 percent of all families in this country—almost one third—were headed by single parents. Primarily caused by divorce, widowhood, and abandonment, single parenting demands are challenging ones. The custodial parent must often cope with loss while assuming increased responsibility, adjusting to a change in role and circumstance while providing continuity of care for children adjusting to changes of their own. In addition, he or she must struggle against a lingering social stigma: a single-parent family constitutes a broken home that provides inadequate care and so produces troubled children.

This social prejudice is as wrong as it is real. However, to the extent that single parents accept this stereotype, they will undercut their confidence with doubt, attack their self-esteem with guilt, and end up indicting themselves for inadequacy no matter how much they care or how hard they try. Not only is all this self-recrimination for no good cause, it can actually reduce the effectiveness of their parenting.

Although it is true that two parents sharing child care within the same home can divide the work and provide mutual support, it is also true that many single mothers and fathers are outstanding parents. By rising to the challenge of great responsibility, they can develop extraordinary strengths, four of which come immediately to mind. First, custodial parents learn to speak directly with their children and make tough rules stick. They know clear communication and firm decisions are what hold the family together. Second, custodial parents learn to manage many different responsibilities and to work efficiently. There is now more variety demanded in their roles and less time to get everything done. Third, custodial parents learn to become more committed parents. They know responsibility for daily child care rests primarily upon them. And fourth, custodial parents learn to give up going it alone. Reaching out to others, they build support on which the family can rely.

This support is absolutely essential because custodial single parents represent a segment of our society who are underserved for the enormous needs and numbers they represent. More than one quarter of all births are to abandoned mothers. Almost half of all marriages with children end in divorce. This high incidence of single parenthood is not a social problem to be solved, but a social reality to be helpfully addressed. The social, emotional, and economic pressures on one-parent families are enormous, but so is the dedication of these custodial mothers and fathers to the welfare of their children.

The purpose of this book is to assist these single parents in the important work they do. Parts One and Two describe the process of transition into single-parent life for the custodial parent and the children. Parts Three and Four recommend priorities to custodial parents for themselves and the new family they are organizing. Parts Five and Six review common factors that can powerfully affect family functioning, anticipating in particular how adolescence typically alters the parent/child relationship. Part Seven examines the impact of the educational system and how custodial parents can help their children successfully advance through school. Parts Eight, Nine, and Ten respectively address the challenges of family management according to significantly different single-parent circumstances: The Divorced Single

Parent, The Widowed Single Parent, and The Abandoned Single Parent.

At the end of the book are ten commonly asked questions, the answers to which have particular importance to single parents; a list of further readings; the names of some helpful support groups; and a glossary defining some terms used in the book that may be unfamiliar. In all cases, unless otherwise noted, the term "single parent" refers to the *custodial* single parent.

1

ADJUSTING TO CHANGE

LETTING GO AND MOVING ON

Entry into single parenthood primarily results from divorce, widowhood, or abandonment. In consequence of these changes, a mother or father is left in a position of sole parenting responsibility. Immediately, his or her role can become dramatically altered as a host of new demands, as caretaker and supporter, are suddenly created. How to master these demands and how to help children with their adjustment is the question. The answer involves progressing through a process of transition that can last up to several years before the journey from an old to a new family reality feels complete. Understanding the nature of transition can help a single parent prepare for, and be patient with, some of the difficulties both the parent and children can encounter.

The first set of adjustments are the most painful ones because they require giving up old relationships that have been lost. The nuclear family broken by divorce, the beloved spouse and parent taken by death, the vanished man who promised love forever until pregnancy occurred; these are all losses that hurt, and this hurt must be addressed.

Giving up powerful emotional connections, however, is not quickly or easily accomplished. Breaking ties takes time.

Consider the resistance of children adjusting to a parent's death. Rather than at first admitting that their parent has died, young children may deny the loss by making believe the parent will magically return. They may resort to *denial* to protect themselves from the pain. This denial does not mean something is wrong with the children. Denial can help delay acknowledgment of pain until children feel emotionally ready to confront the loss that has occurred.

Having admitted the loss, children may still *hold on* to the sense of family that they knew. Instead of letting go, they do what they can to act just like they did when the parent was alive. They may religiously repeat rituals that invoke the departed parent's presence, setting a place at the table should that person magically return. Holding on to some of what is lost helps make admission bearable. At last, having admitted and let go of the loss, children begin to *mourn* their feelings out, actively grieving all they miss. Grieving hurt is how the wound is healed.

Giving up the old is the first half of transition—admitting, letting go, mourning the loss. Overlapping this first phase of adjustment is the second, getting on with the new. Continuing with the example of children recovering from a parent's death, this second phase of transition demands accepting life on different terms than they have known before. Because these terms are unwanted, children may continue to rely on resistance to slow down their adjustment to the change. At first they may reject the terms, refusing to meet some of the new demands placed upon them. *Rejection* buys time until children feel strong enough and ready to begin reaching out, relating, and rebuilding lives that feel like they've been broken.

Having grudgingly accepted their new reality, they may still hold themselves back from fully committing to it out of some lingering loyalty and longing for what was left behind. They may act halfhearted in their attempts to do what is required at home, in social situations, and at school. *Holding back* allows them to practice the motions without yet making a commitment.

At last, having committed themselves to live on life's altered terms, children do achieve an accommodation to their new circumstance. *Accommodation* helps them get settled in. It still takes awhile, however, before they can begin to exploit new opportunities adversity has created, engaging with freedoms that did not exist before. Getting on with the new is the second half of transition—accepting, committing to, and exploiting the change that has revolutionized their lives. In both halves of transition, single parents need to expect and respect resistance to unwanted change from their children.

During the first phase of transition, the single parent gives empathy to children in response to loss. Helping them identify what feels hardest to give up, the single parent talks through what is most missed, as they express and relieve their grief. During the second phase, the single parent gently but firmly enforces the new reality by shifting the focus of discussion to what feels hardest to deal with in the new situation. The single parent talks about these challenges and how to cope with them.

The issues in the first phase of transition tend to be more emotional—how to deal with the pain of breaking old ties. Those in the second phase tend to be more strategic—how to begin making new ties of comparable value. Each is hard in its own way, each person proceeding at his or her own pace, struggling with his or her individual issues. What is difficult for one person, for example, making new friends, may be no problem for another. Yet the second may still cry at night long after the first is done with grieving. Each member of the family needs permission to go through transition in his or her own way. If after two to three years, however, a family member is still deep in struggle with adjustment, that person may be stuck. Then seeking professional counseling can help assist with the completion of the transition.

2

~~~~~~

RESETTING EXPECTATIONS

ANTICIPATING NEW REALITIES

The transition into single parenthood requires adjustments in two directions: giving up old and valued connections to the past, and facing a new and different future. Although moving out of the past can entail grief over what is lost, facing the future requires managing uncertainty about what will happen next.

To reduce fearful ignorance of the unknown, the single parent and the children must create expectations to anticipate the new reality they have entered, to answer the question: "What is our new life going to be like?"

Coping with change from parental divorce, for example, children need to know what they can count on during this period of loss and confusion, particularly in relation to their parents. This is why the single parent can helpfully establish some fixed schedules and routines that children can depend upon for their security. This is also why the noncustodial parent can helpfully establish regular communication and visitation as soon as possible. When their family goes through change, children want to know what they can expect.

Next, it is helpful for the single parent to develop *realistic* expectations about the new situation and the ex-spouse.

This may mean having to accept some changes in both that, although disliked, are beyond the single parent's control. To maintain unrealistic expectations in the face of negative realities that will not go away is harmful. It will invite unnecessary stress into the single parent's already demanding life. Unrealistic expectations can do the single parent emotional injury.

Consider three kinds of expectations:

1. There are *predictions*—what a person believes will happen.
2. There are *ambitions*—what a person wants to have happen.
3 There are *conditions*—what a person believes should happen.

Expectations are mental sets that can have powerful emotional consequences when the reality the single parent encounters is not the one he or she anticipated. Then violations occur, and stress results. Here is how this can transpire.

Suppose the single parent's prediction is that the ex spouse will maintain close and frequent communication with the children. The former partner gets diverted by the pleasures of single living, however, and in consequence the agreed upon contact becomes irregular and unreliable. Children are left waiting for pick-ups that are either late, canceled at the last minute, or forgotten. When the single par ent's prediction is violated, surprise and anxiety follow (as well as anger at a commitment broken and a child's excitement disappointed). This is not what was expected. Now each scheduled visit is preceded by worry over whether it will actually take place If this inconsistency becomes a reality that no amount of persuasion can alter, then the single parent and children need to adjust their expectations accordingly. They need to predict this unreliability to relieve them selves of surprise and anxiety when a visit is delayed or defaulted. Their best prediction is that sometimes the noncustodial parent will pick up as agreed, and sometimes not. Given this uncertainty it is best not to count on the contact. If other opportunities arise, feel free to schedule something else, calling the noncustodial parent to postpone the visit.

Or suppose that the single parent's ambition is that although they are divorced, maybe one day the former partner will have a change of heart and they will reconcile. Getting back together is what the single parent dearly wants. When the ex-spouse announces plans to remarry someone else, however, the single parent's ambition is violated. Disappointment and grief quickly follow. This is not what was expected. Should the single parent let go of this cherished dream for reunion? Yes. When the ex-spouse's remarriage becomes a reality the single parent cannot change, he or she needs to adjust expectations to fit this unhappy turn of events, giving up an unrealizable ambition in order to gain relief from ongoing disappointment.

Or suppose the single parent's condition is that child support payments from the noncustodial parent should be timely and unbroken. Then the noncustodial parent loses a job, adjusts to subsisting on occasional employment, and stops sending any money to help out. Or perhaps financial contributions stop for no identifiable reason. When the single parent's condition is violated, betrayal and anger follow. It feels infuriating that the other parent should give up all financial responsibility for the children. This is not what was expected. This is not right! However, if despite urgings and even legal action the noncustodial parent stubbornly refuses to find regular employment or resume payments, even willing to go to jail for being delinquent, the single parent needs to relinquish a condition that will not be met. Letting the old condition go is done not to relieve the ex-spouse of responsibility, but to relieve the single parent of ongoing anger in response to nonsupport. Should the noncustodial parent ever resume reliable employment, then that condition may legally be enforced by wages becoming garnered. Now the noncustodial parent is being made to contribute as he or she should.

Because the emotional consequences of violated expectations are so powerful, it is also useful for the single parent to help children set their own expectations in a realistic way. This can be done by asking the children three simple questions:

1. What do you think will happen now that we are divorced (what are your predictions)?
2. What do you want to have happen now that we are divorced (what are your ambitions)?
3. How do you think arrangements should work now that we are divorced (what are your conditions)?

By asking these questions, expectations can be clarified in two ways. First, the single parent can help dispel those that are unrealistic and not likely to be met. "I know you want us to get back together some day, but that is simply not a possibility." And second, the children may share some expectations that the single parent didn't know about that one or the other parent can fulfill. "Yes," promises the noncustodial parent, "we can get you a bed here just like the one you have at home."

The most important expectations for the custodial father or mother to keep realistic are those concerning his or her own performance as a parent. Beware unrealistic expectations like "I *will* meet all my children's needs," "I *want* to make my children always well behaved," "I *should* please my children to prove myself a good parent." Rather than striving for such idealistic expectations, the single parent is better served by giving to himself or herself expectations of acceptance: "I will do what I can," "I want what I have," and "I should be as I am."

Expectations are not fixed, nor genetic. They are chosen. Self-expectations of perfection create enormous stress because the single parent strives so hard and fails so often. Much of the time, he or she lives in a state of violation feeling anxious, grief stricken, or angry. So the moral is: treat yourself to *expectations of acceptance*. Choose expectations that fit the reality of who you are, how you are able to live, and what you can realistically accomplish.

3

MANAGING GRIEVANCE

THE CONSTRUCTIVE AND DESTRUCTIVE
USE OF ANGER

Anger may not be an enjoyable emotion, but it is a functional one. Anger patrols an individual's sense of well-being. It identifies violations by making judgments: "that is unfair," "that hurts," "that's wrong," "that should not have happened." Anger empowers a person to make three important reactions: an *expressive* response to violation by airing grievances, a *protective* response to violation by setting boundaries and limits, and a *corrective* response to violation by asserting demands for change. All these reactions are made for the self-perceived preservation of a secure and just interaction in relationship.

People who can't feel anger, or can't allow themselves to get angry directly, are in danger of being undefended when mistreatment occurs. They are at risk of accepting the unacceptable without awareness or opposition, and of suffering in silence when injuries occur. More important, by not acknowledging or expressing anger, they may encourage mistreatment to continue by keeping the errant party in ignorance of the wrong being committed. Thus, by not saying anything to a mid-adolescent child who freely borrows parental belongings without asking and returns them damaged or not at all, the parent only enables this unacceptable behavior to continue. The infuriated mother or father complains loudly to friends, but never angrily confronts the offending teenager for fear of causing yet another argument between them.

Anxious questions can keep people from expressing honest anger. Is the other person going to get angry back? Is the other person going to feel hurt? Is the relationship going to become strained, conflicted, or distant in response to anger's impact? Because the answer to these questions may be "yes," every person has to weigh the costs of expressing anger against the costs of holding it in. If one cost of keeping anger secret is keeping the other person in ignorance, another is allowing anger to stressfully accumulate until overreaction to small frustrations becomes likely to occur. People prone to temper are frequently those who do not keep emotionally current with their anger, ignoring or denying irritation at the time, storing it up for later misuse.

Typically, the management of anger is learned in one's family of origin through *how* that emotion is modeled, encouraged, and allowed by the adults in charge. Because single parents are creating the family of origin for their children, as fathers and mothers they need to example and instruct how anger can be usefully expressed so their children can *learn* to manage anger well. Continually losing their temper and yelling criticism at a child for a mistake or misdeed may teach the child that anger should be forcefully and hurtfully directed. By never showing or allowing anger in the family, however, parents may imply that the emotion is unacceptable and should therefore be suppressed. Between these two extremes single parents need to find a middle way—the constructive use of anger—safely talking about felt violations when they occur. "When you don't do as you promise, I feel angry because I can't count on you to keep your word."

In single-parent families, learning to honor and constructively express feelings of anger is extremely important. When a partner dies, when a parent is abandoned, or when a divorce occurs, some grievance is commonly experienced.

There is some anger at an unwanted, unexpected, or undeserved turn of events. Consider the case of divorce.

For most children, parental divorce feels like a broken promise. They assumed that Mother and Father would stay married forever. Violate that assumption and children will feel some degree of anger. Divorce isn't fair. It isn't right. "If my parents weren't planning to stay together then they shouldn't have had kids!" Parents have to be willing to nondefensively hear this anger out.

Parents have their angers too. Because it is a corrective response to a marriage that feels unworkable for at least one partner, divorce is a decision partly fueled by grievances from injuries sustained over the history of the relationship. Without some anger, few couples can reach a meaningful divorce; yet by remaining angry thereafter, most couples cannot emotionally close out the relationship and freely go their separate ways. In living through divorce, there is a time to get angry and a time to put anger to rest.

In divorce, anger can serve three constructive functions:

1. It can allow each partner to identify those grievances that they have experienced in marriage, and, thus, meaningfully communicate the unhappiness each feels. Anger can cite some of the grounds for divorce.
2. It can energize conflict that clarifies those differences that both partners are unwilling to accept, but are unable to negotiate.
3. If partially and nonabusively expressed in front of the children, anger can provide honest evidence of discord. Children need to know that some significant unhappiness exists between their mother and father that has nothing to do with them.

This last function is important because when children are totally protected from parental discord, divorce can

come as a total surprise. "But we never _____
with each other! We never saw you fight or _____
must be something else. It must be us."

Anger can also serve destructive functi_____
as an excuse to justify doing emotional o_____
When parents confide their anger at each other to get the child
on one or the other's side, the child can feel torn apart by con-
flicting loyalties. At worst, by resorting to revenge, an embittered partner may commit to getting the other back by using
the children as unwitting weapons in a war of reprisal. When
this occurs, the worst injury is to the children. As for the
parental perpetrator, revenge does not relieve his or her anger.
Revenge just keeps resentment at old wounds alive.

As for extended mutual bitterness after the marriage
has been ended, that only shows the divorce is not complete.
Neither partner has grown emotionally free of the other, both
are holding on. Truthfully, they will declare their love is over;
but falsely they will offer this truth as evidence that their old
connection is at an end. Not so. Love and hate are both pas-
sionate attachments. They have only substituted one emotional tie for another. They are still married: in anger.

The single parent needs to discriminate between _getting
angry_ (and doing something affirmative to mend or recover
from the violation) and _staying angry_ (but doing nothing
except dwelling on past wrongs that are beyond correcting).
To let the former spouse live "rent-free" in one's head by har-
boring resentments against that person costs the noncustodial parent no immediate discomfort, but burdens the
custodial parent with an ongoing emotional preoccupation. It
is better to liberate one's energy and life by letting old grievances and angers go.

If after a year or so of self-searching and talking with
confidantes about injuries from the marriage and divorce, the

parent is still fixated on old grievances, then joining a
ce recovery group or getting individual counseling may
helpful to finish the reluctant work of letting anger go.

Anger work can be extremely hard if one was the recipi-
ent of mistreatment from abuse, addiction, infidelity, or
other exploitation. Help required in these cases includes
making an inventory not only of angers at the ex-spouse, but
also of angers at oneself for allowing the treatment to go on.
This anger at oneself can be valuable because it can help the
single parent make a promise: "To the degree I was responsible for letting this happen, I will *never* put myself at the
effect of such mistreatment again." Then anger can make
another vow: "I will not waste any more time and emotion on
my ex-spouse and his or her offenses, but will invest all my
energy in making a better life for the children and myself."
Anger can help bring self-destructive behaviors to an end.

4

~~~~~~

OBJECTING TO UNWANTED CHANGE

UNDERSTANDING EMOTIONAL PROTEST AND RESISTANCE

Although most mothers or fathers do not expect their children to welcome parental death, divorce, or abandonment, many are still surprised by the amount of *protest* and *resistance* their son or daughter expresses.

Through protest, children ventilate their hurts and angers over what has been lost. Through resistance, they oppose adjustments demanded by the new family situation. Both protest and resistance responses are natural parts of children's adjustment to a change they didn't anticipate, do not want, but must eventually accept.

The single parent needs to be prepared for both responses, understanding he or she will be the major outlet for emotional upset and target for opposition. One key to preparation is for the single parent *not* to wait for the protest and resistance to emerge, but to regularly invite out their discussion. By taking this initiative, the single parent can actually channel children's hurt feelings and objections, at the same time providing evidence of ongoing caring and support. Key questions to keep asking are: "How are you *feeling* about the change?" and "What *adjustments* do you wish you did not have to make?"

15

In divorce, the noncustodial parent is often spared protest and resistance behaviors because that parent is not constantly around. When there is visitation contact, children often do not want to strain their relationship with a parent whom they now only occasionally see.

Dealing with Protest

Emotional protest in children takes some common forms:

- The child can express fear by worrying: "What will happen to me now?"
- The child can express suffering by grieving: "I am in pain over what has been lost."
- The child can express anger by charging: "It's not fair for this to happen."
- The child can express helplessness by complaining: "I am a victim of events I can't control."
- The child can hold the custodial parent accountable with blame: "It's all your fault!"

Helpfully listening to these emotions requires the single parent to exercise some self-restraint by not interrupting, not correcting, not criticizing, and not trying to fix hurt feelings that are being expressed. Listening conveys acceptance of the pain. There comes a time, however, to limit listening as well. If toward the end of the first year children are still venting earlier protests of fear, anger, suffering, helplessness, or blame without gaining apparent relief or making additional headway, then listening may be protracting protest and not advancing their adjustment. Ritual repetition of the child's unhappiness may have become an end in itself, draining off precious energy and delaying constructive action. At this point, the single parent may want to listen less and demand more. "It's time to stop giving all your energy to feeling hurt. You need to start focusing on what you can do to make yourself happy." If the child still cannot move on, then professional counseling may be advised.

Dealing with Resistance

Resistance is simply the act of saying "no" to an external demand. Expressed actively by spoken opposition, or passively by silent refusal, resistance is an act of power that asserts limits to what a person will agree to do. Because children experience a significant loss of control over their lives when a parent is partially or completely lost, resistance is often how they seek to regain some sense of power.

A single parent can support this important recovery of power by making concessions.

- Children can be given their say (allowed to voice objections), but the single parent, having listened, can still get his or her way (insisting on compliance).
- Children can be given some room to refuse before they consent to comply.
- Children can be given time for delay before doing what they have been told.
- Children can be given choices within the larger choice the single parent has made.

During the early stages of transition into single-parent family life, these concessions give children some sense of control in a situation where they feel power has been stripped away. Each of these concessions also ends with the single parent hanging tough to get what he or she needs to have happen. As time passes and transition is accomplished, resistance to change subsides as the new reality is gradually accepted and children become more tractable again.

For some single parents, making concessions with this early resistance feels wrong because in doing so they believe they will be sacrificing authority. Authority need not be

KEYS TO SINGLE PARENTING

absolute to be effective, however. Parents can allow themselves some leeway. They can negotiate at the point of resistance, coming out with a compromise: "I will let you put off doing this right now, if you will commit to do it later, by an agreed upon time." Respecting resistance respects the child's need for self-control. Keeping his or her side of the bargain teaches the child some responsibility for cooperation. Both the single parent and the child can be well served by such agreements.

5

^^^

STILL SUFFERING

BEING PATIENT WITH YOUR CHILD'S PAIN

O f high priority for single parents after spousal death, divorce, or abandonment is stabilizing the new family structure and helping children recover from the hard change that has taken place. In addition, single parents want to get on with their own lives. They hunger for a better time, and they want children to want that too. Unhappily, one or more of the children may not be in the same state of readiness that they are. Although a single parent can be reaching for a better future, a child can be dwelling on a broken past. This difference creates an incompatibility between them in the present.

The child seems to declare: "I am not yet ready to let go my longing for the family that I had." In response, the single parent may become impatient: "Here I am ready to get on with our new life together, but you keep dragging us back to memories of the old one that you miss." In this opposition, neither one is in a good position to sympathize with the other because they differ over *timing*.

How can this happen? Consider the example of a divorce, where the single parent was the partner who initiated ending the marriage. In this situation, he or she has had a head start dealing with the transition that the child has not. After all, the single parent's adjustment began when he or she first questioned the marriage, contemplated leaving it, and began to imagine how life alone with the children would be. In this process, he or she worked through a lot of pain well before the child first learned about the forthcoming divorce. This lag in adjustment time means the single parent simply has to be patient as the aggrieved child works through many hurts and gradually catches up to the parent's acceptance of family change.

Repetition Is Necessary

The child's recurrent complaints require parental understanding about the importance of repeated grieving when working through a loss. Just as with the death of a loved one, a single episode of mourning is insufficient to discharge all the grief. With each repetition of unhappiness that may seem excessive and irritating to the parent, the child is incrementally discharging pain, and gradually gaining more acceptance and relief upon which full adjustment shall finally depend. The single parent may find it difficult to see repetition as a path of progress, but progress it is.

Listening can feel additionally hard when the single parent feels implicated in the child's suffering, such as in the parental choice of divorce. However, to become defensive ("It's *not* all my fault!") or guilty ("It's all my fault!") only compounds the problem. Defensiveness may discourage the child from further expression because he or she wasn't looking for an argument. As for parental guilt, responding to this may divert the child from his or her own pain to comfort or assure the tormented adult.

Putting Responsibility in Its Place

Just because the single parent had the power to initiate divorce, thereby causing the children pain, doesn't mean he or she has the power to heal that pain. "Since I caused it, I can cure it" is a false assumption because it oversteps the bounds of the single parent's power of responsibility. Only the child can heal himself or herself. At most, the single parent can help the child by patiently listening and by exploring the positive possibilities that family change has created.

What possibilities? There are two kinds:

1. There are *freedoms from* old constraints that may have been attached to how the absent parent wanted the family constructed and conducted. Some of these demands and limits may no longer apply.
2. There are also *freedoms for* fresh opportunities, like room to initiate new interests and enjoyments that did not exist before.

Hearing out a son or daughter's pain and enabling positive possibilities are how the single parent can help the child who is struggling with adjustment.

6

~~~~~~

INSECURITIES

COPING WITH THE FEARS THAT LOSS CREATES

Parental death or divorce can create fear of the future for the young child, fear of the unknown. Having lost one parent to death, the young child may worry about losing the other. When a parent dies, the child's world feels unsafe. Divorce also creates fear—fear of abandonment. The child may wonder: "If my father and mother can leave each other, can they also leave me?" In the face of these uncertainties, the child may regress by acting more insecure and dependent. He or she may cling to the single parent who is now the only full-time parent left.

Regularly, for example, a four-year-old consigned to an older child while the single parent takes an evening walk may caution the departing mother or father: "Watch out for cars, don't get lost, don't die, come back soon, and don't forget that!"

Young children may suddenly find being dropped off at day care or school frightening. They may be reluctant to let the parent go, lest he or she not return to pick them up or not be there when the child gets home. The single parent needs to counter this temporary insecurity with reassurances, being willing to answer the same questions day after day as long as the child confronts the same fears. Over time, the recitation of these answers can become a kind of comforting ritual to help the child bridge these necessary separations. Departure and reunion rituals of this kind are important for the parent to support. They are the child's way of structuring safe passage through a time of uncertainty and fear.

Besides rituals, routines can also help quell fears. A predictable organization of daily life becomes supportive. Knowing what structure to expect when living with the custodial parent and knowing the schedule of visitation with a noncustodial mother or father provide security on which the child can depend. The anxious child of divorce needs to be assured that even though the marriage is over, he or she still has some parental figure to count on. Therefore, answer questions patiently, establish rituals and routines, establish reliable visitation, and do not criticize or punish the child for being afraid. Fear needs to be talked out, not driven into concealment by parental disapproval, hidden by the child's embarrassment or shame.

With adolescent children, the entry into single-parent family living through divorce can come at a bad time. Just when the teenager is awakening to yearnings for enduring romance, he or she is confronted with the impermanence of love. At best, young love is a scary proposition, fraught with risk of injury from being hurt and getting rejected. For these reasons, many teenagers want to make love safe by believing that once established it will last. Parental divorce at this time raises a host of disturbing questions. "If my parents can lose love for each other, does that mean that love is not forever?" "If love can die, how can it sicken or get killed?" "If death of love is so painful, is it better to stay out of love and avoid getting hurt?" To see parental love ending when their own ideals about love are just beginning can be disillusioning for adolescents.

Sometimes teenagers will withdraw from the possibility of love in their own relationships because of parental divorce. Fearing the fragility of love, they may resist close-ness and commitment, keeping involvement safe by keeping it superficial, partying to keep from getting personal. Or they may decide only to accept caring relationships where they are in firm control and feel emotionally secure.

When the death of a parent coincides with a child's ado-lescence, this event may also cause teenagers to distance themselves from caring relationships. Fears of mortality can get in the way. If a loved one can die at any moment, maybe it is less painful not to love. The threat of death can also cause them to reassess the meaning of life. They may ques-tion the point of purpose and commitment. Is it worthwhile to care?

In response to these natural doubts, it can be helpful for the single parent to talk with their teenagers about the risks and rewards of love in the wake of parental death or divorce. The single mother or father does not need to be an expert on love in general, only on his or her own view in particular. There are no right or easy answers. Discussion is what needs to happen. The son or daughter needs opportunity to reassess his or her view of love and life, given the loss that has occurred.

7

‸‸‸

CHANGING PARENTS

GETTING USED TO A PARENT
BECOMING DIFFERENT

For many children, when their parent is widowed, divorced, or abandoned, the changes have just begun. Freed from old constraints of the marriage and faced with new demands, the single parent begins to grow and change as an individual. Sometimes these changes can be quite dramatic.

For example, when divorce feels like a release from years of personal confinement, preoccupation with personal growth can be extremely self-absorbing. The single parent may approach this new freedom with a sense of entitlement: "I deserve a chance to do what I've always wanted and have never been allowed." Socially, occupationally, educationally, emotionally, spiritually, intellectually, physically, in any of these ways, the single parent begins to expand his or her traditional definition. As alterations occur, these changes can be jarring to the bewildered child. "It's like seeing your parent behaving like a stranger!"

Confronted by differences that are not understood, the child feels ignorant and may become *anxious*. "What's going on?" Feeling put off by the parent's new attitudes and behaviors, the child may long for the old familiar relationship and feel *lonely*: "I miss the way my parent used to be." Having to adjust to new parental conduct and priorities that the child neither wants nor likes, he or she may become resentful and feel *angry*: "Why should I have to change my life just because my parent wants to change?"

Now the potential for parent/child conflict arises. Acting out of ignorance and anxiety, the child may ask questions that the parent finds uncomfortable or intrusive. "I don't have to explain to you my every action!" Acting out of loneliness for the old way of being together, the child may try to hold the parent back in ways the mother or father finds threatening. "I have a right to lead my own life and you are not going to stop me!" Acting out of resentment and anger at having to adjust to parental changes, the child may criticize in ways the parent finds offensive. "It's not your place to judge how I conduct my life!"

Rather than let the relationship become at odds over the parent's need to grow, the single parent can be attentive to how his or her changes are affecting the child. The parent can do this by asking certain helpful questions: "What information do you need about the changes I am making in my life? What can I tell you? What do you miss from our old relationship? How can we stay close to each other? Which changes that I'm making are making life hard for you? How can I help make those changes easier for you?"

One change the single parent must discuss is when he or she starts dating, because the implications for children are too important to ignore. For younger children, make it very clear that early dating is social and recreational, satisfying a need for adult companionship. Should it ever become serious and romantic, fulfilling the parent's need for adult love, then the children should be told that this is now a significant relationship. Be careful about including children on a social date because they may assume the relationship is serious when it is not. Should they begin to develop affection and become attached to the parent's companion, a breakup of that relationship may bring them disappointment and another experience of loss.

For teenage children, parental dating raises additional concerns. At a time when they are coming into their own sexuality and beginning dating, now their parent has become a sexual and dating person too. This can be threatening. "My parent is acting my age!" This can be embarrassing. "My friends think it's funny that I have a parent who dates!" This can be worrisome. "How do I know the person whom my parent is dating is safe to be with?"

The single parent who has begun to date needs to talk with young children about the difference between social and serious dating. With adolescent children, he or she needs to discuss how to conduct parental dating in such a way that the teenagers can grow comfortable with this new behavior.

8

~~~~~~

TAKING CHARGE

ASSERTING POWER TO REGAIN CONTROL

Loss of a parent, whether through death, divorce, or abandonment, is experienced by children as a loss of power. Either impersonal fate or parental choice, neither of which children control, has drastically altered their lives. In response, they often want to compensate by getting control back, reasserting power in some ways the single parent can support, but in other ways he or she must oppose.

Consider the example of divorce. By mutual agreement, parents end their marriage in the hopes that separate lives will bring them less misery, more happiness, or both. An act of power on the part of parents, divorce is usually not the child's desire and is never the child's choice. Most children want their parents to stay together. Now the family unit upon which the child assumed he or she could depend is divided by parents acting out of self-interest, placing parental happiness ahead of what their children want.

Perceiving parental divorce in these self-centered terms, it is not uncommon for a child to become more dedicated to his or her own self-interest in return. This becomes most apparent when divorce coincides with the child's adolescence—that process of separation from childhood that typically begins between the ages of nine and thirteen. Divorce tends to intensify adolescence. It can drive many normal tendencies of growth at this stage to extremes. The sense of grievance, the negativity, the resistance, the early experimentation, the preoccupation with friends, the lack of communication at home, and the push for freedom can all become more pronounced. At this time of life, *contrast* (asserting differentness from childhood and parents), *opposition* (testing and contesting authority), and *independence* (seeking social freedom from family) are leading themes in the child's growth. The single parent needs to anticipate that divorce may cause these themes to be more strongly played than if the marriage had remained happily intact.

All growth is a gathering of power. The parent's task is to help children gather it in appropriate, not inappropriate ways. Thus, even young children may try to exploit divorce to increase their sense of influence. For example, they may try to exploit differences between households to their advantage. "If I'm allowed to stay up late and watch TV over there, why can't I do that over here?" The child is simply trying to import freedom permitted in one home back into the other. In response, the single parent needs to have an answer to this ploy. "Now you have to live by *two* sets of family rules, not just by one. There will be differences between the households, and the inconsistencies will take some getting used to. On visitation, you do things their way. At home, you do them mine."

Most commonly, children of divorce will push for power where they sense the parent is easily influenced or feels insecure. They may use manipulation to get their way. They may try to overcome parental limits or demands with *emotional extortion.* For example, the child may use *affection* to soften up the single parent by appealing to his or her *need for love.* After all, it can feel hard to deny a child who is acting his or her hugging, darling best. Or the child may use the expression of *anger* to intimidate the single parent who has a *fear of rejection.* Expressed loudly or silently, the child's anger may drive the parent to relent just to gain relief from his or her anxiety. There are numerous tactics to sway a parent from a firm refusal or a fixed stand:

- If the parent is *susceptible to pity*, the child can use the expression of *helplessness.*
- If the parent is *prone to guilt*, the child can use the expression of *suffering.*
- If the parent *dreads abandonment*, the child can use the expression of *apathy.*
- If the single parent is *scared of physical harm*, the child can use *violence.*
- If a single mother or father is *worried about loss*, the son or daughter can *threaten to leave* and go live with the other parent.

All these emotional manipulations are inappropriate ways for the child to gather power, and the single parent needs to deny them. Emotional extortion destroys trust, discourages rational discussion, and creates resentment. It exploits vulnerability. At its worst, it can corrupt the expression of true feeling. Thus the next time his or her emotionally manipulative child authentically bursts into tears, instead of sympathizing with the pain, the single parent cynically asks: "All right, what is it you want this time?"

To discourage these efforts at manipulation, the single parent needs to model the *declaration* of needs instead, demanding declaration in return. "After you are through acting angry, tell me what it is you want or do not want to have happen and we can talk about it." When the single parent refuses to be driven by emotional extortion, then the game becomes not worth playing for the child.

Finally, there are positive parental approaches for helping children reassert their diminished sense of power. Give the child a share in some family responsibilities he or she wants to take. Solicit ideas he or she may have for restructuring the single-parent family. Wherever possible, give choices within the larger parental choice of what the child is being asked to do. "This is what I need to have happen. Tell me what would be the best way for you to get it done." To the degree that the single parent can initiate positive means for children to gather power, they may be less inclined to push for the negative ones.

9

~~~~~~

REBUILDING

MODERATING START-UP DEMANDS

A trap is set for some single parents, particularly those who have recently divorced. The name of that trap is *freedom*. Recently liberated from a marriage in which happiness felt sorely lacking and much hardship was endured, they may resolve to make up for what they missed now that they are single. Feeling deprived in the past, they want to compensate in the present. In doing so, they run a risk. Satisfying just *some* of their frustrated longings may feel insufficient. Only excess seems enough to make up for what was lacking or denied. They want it *all*, and they want it *now*. Only extremes will do.

They may want to socialize in the extreme to compensate for years of isolation. They may want to exercise in the extreme to compensate for years of being sedentary and depressed. They may want to enroll in endless self-improvement activities to compensate for years of self-neglect. Although all these involvements may be affirming, they can become too much of a good thing when pursued at the expense of meeting basic family commitments.

Family demands have already increased because there is one less parent in the residence to manage household responsibilities. If, in addition to this adjustment, the single parent invests in excessive personal change, he or she can overtax existing energy and stress will result.

It is hard to moderate one's appetite after feeling starved because the pangs of hunger and dreams of satiation are so strong. However, *moderation* is the key for stabilizing the single parent who feels liberated by spousal death, abandonment, or divorce. It takes restraint to go slow when the temptations of new possibilities are urging full speed ahead. As one single parent aptly put it: "After the divorce, I wanted more than was good for me. I had to learn not to go too fast."

Speed of the single parent's life can be roughly calculated by resorting to that formula he or she probably learned back in elementary school: *rate* of speed = *distance / time.* Change the distance variable into *demand,* and the speed with which a single parent is living can be estimated by assessing the number of demands to be satisfied in relation to the amount of time available to get them met. The more demands, the less time, the faster or harder the single parent must push himself or herself to get everything done. To slow down, either reduce the number of demands, increase the time allotted, or do both. More specifically, to regulate his or her speed of life, the single parent must learn to manage three important controls: goals, standards, and limits.

Goals have to do with achievement. How much does the single parent want to accomplish and how soon does that parent want to get it all done? If, within the first year after divorce, he or she wants to lose substantial weight, find a meaningful relationship, occupationally retrain by going back to school a few nights a week, and get a better job, he or she has committed to a very high speed of life. This is a lot to accomplish in a short time. High ambition can create a high speed of life.

Standards have to do with excellence. How well does the single parent want to do all the time? If the single father or mother decides to apply a standard of perfection to everything he or she does, whether at home, with the children, or at work, an impossible ideal becomes the measure for what is good enough. There is no room for inconsistency, error, or ordinary performance. Less than impeccability is considered failure. Perfection is a human standard that can exert inhuman pressure on those who choose to serve it. They must lead a high speed of life to keep from falling short of the harsh criterion that they have set.

Limits have to do with tolerance. How much can the single parent do at one time? If the single parent strives to satisfy every demand that the children make to make them happy, he or she is likely to make them even more demanding. By satisfying every desire, others are encouraged. The more the children get, the more they expect. The more they expect, the more they want. The more they want, the more they demand. The more the single parent tries to keep up with this demand, the more exhausted he or she becomes. Letting children set a parent's limits soon becomes overwhelming, and a high speed of life results.

Starting up a single-parent family, a mother or father is well advised to go slow. Discipline yourself to think about how much demand is enough for a given amount of time. One helpful exercise is to make three lists:

1. In the first, specify *maximum* goals, standards, and limits that you would love to live by.
2. In the second, itemize the *minimum* goals, standards, and limits that would allow you barely to get by.
3. In the third, chart a middle range, describing a *moderate* set of goals, standards, and limits that would provide sufficiency without excess.

Instead of full speed ahead, the single parent is advised to go at a *deliberate speed*, where some is enough, imperfection is human, and failing to satisfy every want is okay.

10

^^^

COPING WITH STRESS

KEEPING THE COSTS FROM SPREADING

Overdemand is a continuing reality and constant problem for single parents. There always seems more that needs doing than they can get done. By overdoing in response, however, they risk depleting their energy to the point where ability to cope requires the assistance of stress.

Stress is an invaluable and endangering capacity. On the positive side, it can be a lifesaving response, enabling people to survive extreme demands they ordinarily could not. On the negative side, however, it can be a life-threatening response by causing people to act destructively to themselves and others from duress. Single parents need to rely on stress selectively. They must guard against its negative consequences for themselves and their children.

Consider how stress can arise. For every demand placed upon human beings by the world and by themselves, people must expend some unit of energy in response. Energy is one's potential for action, and it is *limited*. People do not possess an infinite amount of this precious life resource.

In the case of single parents, as long as the demands upon them remain less than, or equivalent to, their readily available supply of energy, they will feel okay. When the demands exceed what they can readily give, however, then they feel *not* okay. Now the opportunity for stress has been created in the form of two threatening questions: "Can I meet this overdemand? And if I can't, what will happen then?"

In consequence, single parents find themselves confronting a personal energy crisis. To meet what feels like an overdemand, they will have to put themselves into emergency energy production. Using force of will (determination and discipline) and perhaps the assistance of chemicals (sugar, caffeine, or other stimulants) to impel themselves into action, they decide to stress their system to survive.

For example, motivated by urgency, fortified by resolve, stimulated by a cup of coffee, and energized by a candy snack, the single parent gives up the first moment of relaxation he or she has had since getting home to meet a child's emergency. Rushing across town, the tired mother or father borrows the outline for a project that the child forgot, just now remembered, and must hand in tomorrow. And so begins a long night of supervision after a long day at the job.

To rely on stress occasionally like this creates a short-term cost. To meet demands at the office the next day will require more forcing energy, because he or she feels depleted from the prior night. But what happens if reliance on stress becomes constant, not just occasional? Then, predictably, more serious costs begin to be sustained. These costs mount over time because the effects of protracted stress are additive, one level overlaying on the next.

1. Stress on level one is experienced as *fatigue.* "I feel worn-out all the time."
2. Beyond fatigue, the second level of stress is *pain.* "Some part of my body has begun to hurt or feel unwell."
3. Beyond pain, the third level of stress is *burnout.* "It seems like I just don't care anymore."

4. Beyond burnout, the fourth level of stress is *breakdown*. "I just can't get myself to function anymore."

Not only can chronic stress become extremely disabling for the person afflicted, its effects can be contagious to others. Children often feel the impact of the stress the single parent undergoes. Fatigue can make the single parent more negative and critical. Pain can make the single parent oversensitive to small problems and easily irritable. Burnout can make the single parent insensitive and nonresponsive. And breakdown can make the single parent nonfunctional and unavailable. All these effects can occur because stress is not simply self-contained, it is catching. If the single parent pays the costs of constant stress, so shall the children. Upset by their parent's negativity, irritability, nonresponsiveness, or unavailability, children will likely increase demands upon their mother or father, thereby creating more stress in response.

But what choices do single parents have? Stress, like all difficult human problems, has no easy solutions, only hard ones. In this case, the solutions have names: saying "no," and saying "yes." These two little words can help regulate demands and renew energy. By saying "no" to themselves, single parents can resist the temptation of positive possibilities. There are a multitude of ways they could enhance their lives, yet each way creates one more source of demands to meet. Sometimes invitations must be refused and opportunities forgone because single parents have too much demand going on already. They would love to do more, but they physically can't afford the additional expense of energy.

Resisting others can be even more difficult. By saying "no" to a demanding child, parents may well face a negative response. The frustrated son or daughter may express disappointment, argue, or get angry. "You never let me!" "You have no good reason!" "That's not fair!" "You don't love me!"

Against the emotional costs of receiving these complaints, single parents have to weigh the stress of giving in and doing more than they can physically afford. Parenting, particularly single parenting, is not a popularity contest. There are times when single mothers and fathers must deny their child to preserve themselves, to the displeasure of their son or daughter. Saying "no" is how people set limits on demands from themselves and others. To have no limits, or to let other people set one's limits, is to court constant stress.

Saying "yes" to oneself to gratify an important need or want can feel selfish because, in fact, it is. Without *responsible selfishness*, however, single parents will not adequately attend their own health and well-being. Thus, capacity to provide for their children can be put at risk. Whether from sacrifice or guilt, parental self-neglect is in nobody's best interest. Without investing in his or her own upkeep and renewal, any mother or father will eventually run down. To adequately care for your children, take adequate care of yourself. As a reminder of this priority, remember the airline's safety instructions: "*Before* you place the oxygen mask on the child, make sure your own mask is *first* secured."

There is another kind of "yes" that also needs saying; this one is to children. A single parent needs to be able to say "yes, thank you" when they offer to help, and "yes, you will" when they have been asked and resist. In the first instance, this may feel like imposing; in the second, it may feel like courting conflict. In both instances, the issue is the same: for children to share in household work that must be done, and to help out the single parent when needed.

The moral is: If single parents want to keep stress from ruling their lives, they must learn to limit demands, they must enlist the aid of children, and they must give high priority to their own self-maintenance and renewal.

11

‸‸

SELF-MAINTENANCE

CARING ENOUGH TO TAKE CARE OF ONESELF

If one entry into stress in the single parent's life is through overdemand, the other is through self-neglect. In the first case, energy is overspent; in the second, it is undernourished. Without renewal, energy (one's potential for action) runs down, and without energy nothing can get to happen. Keeping his or her energy in good supply, therefore, becomes an ongoing challenge for the single parent.

How is this to be done? Consider two major ways that energy is spent. The first is on *maintenance* activities. Maintenance means fulfilling recurring needs and wants that are essential for people to be able to move from one day to the next feeling good about themselves, with a full complement of energy at their disposal. Maintenance is self-care. It includes a multitude of basic life-support activities: eating regularly and well, sleeping enough, earning money, maintaining adequate hygiene, keeping house, relaxing, caring for the family, and many others. There are so many of these essential activities, in fact, that if they were all enumerated, perhaps as much as 90 percent of what one needs to accomplish each day could be considered part of maintenance. Because it takes such an enormous outlay of energy just to self-maintain, one would think most people would place a high priority on assuring energy sufficiency, yet they do not.

How often does someone say to a single parent: "Congratulations, you've just made it through another day!"

The answer is, not very frequently. Why? Because society tends not to reward people for maintaining themselves. Maintenance is taken for granted, something people are just expected to do. Thus, when a single mother was interviewed about what she had accomplished over the weekend, this hardworking parent disparagingly replied: "Nothing, I just caught up on the basics." Wrong. Taking care of the basics needs to be treated as something *important*. Unless maintenance is recognized and rewarded for the vital contribution it makes, it is in danger, particularly during periods of high demand, of being discounted and ignored. Should this omission occur, it is to the single parent's cost.

For example, when urgency at work and an ill child at home coincide to create peak demand, the single parent may act as though self-maintenance is dispensable. By substituting nonnutritious snacks for a more adequate diet, skipping meals, cutting out relaxing, shortening sleep, and omitting exercises designed to meet a chronic need, the single parent soon becomes unable to sustain sufficient energy when energy is needed most. In consequence, he or she is forced to rely on stress to cope with the emergency. Minimum daily maintenance is most important during periods of maximum demand. Self-care is essential for survival. Yet we live in a culture that extols a higher priority for spending energy.

It is hard to honor the importance of maintenance in a society that rewards another investment in energy more—participating in *change*. Consider the value sets that support these two different ways of spending energy. *Change values* emphasize doing more, new, different, better, and faster. Change is exciting, and by following change values, progress can be gained and success achieved. Not only that, change values are continually sold to the public by an extremely persuasive form of social communication—commercial advertising. Exploiting people's susceptibility to dissatisfaction with who and how they are, and what they have and want, various products and services, and conveniences and opportunities are constantly being promoted because they are *new*, will do *more*, are *different*, will do the job *better*, and will get it done *faster*.

By comparison, *maintenance values* have more modest, less glamorous objectives, and so receive far less popular support. They emphasize doing the old, the same, as well, less than, and slowing down. Maintenance is associated with moderation and stability, with gratitude and contentment. Recovering from the self-destructive effects of excessive striving and inadequate self-care, patients are often given a self-maintenance prescription. Their doctor may advise: "*slow* down, consider cutting back and doing *less*, take the time to keep healthy *old* habits going, commit to continuing the *same* recuperative care you are receiving now, and instead of pushing to constantly do better, relax, be content to do *as well*."

Both maintenance and change are important to the single parent's well-being, but they must be kept *in balance*. If about 90 percent of a person's energy is required for maintenance, that only leaves about 10 percent available for change. This can be a hard balance to keep, however, in a society where change is rewarded and maintenance is not. The temptations of change can be very great.

For example, consider the hypothetical case of Robert. A year past widowhood, with two children, he is finally maintaining personal and family needs when an offer is made for a promotion at work. His immediate response is: "I should take it. It's a *new* position, *more* money, *different* responsibilities, a *better* opportunity, and I'll move up *faster*." The rewards of change are tangible and real; however, so are the costs. To accept the promotion, he will have to invest in change at the expense of maintenance. In doing so, he risks inviting stress into his family's life. After accepting the promotion, change begins to take its toll: longer hours, take-home work, additional worries, less time for self-care, and more irritability with the children. As his son and daughter become anxious and increase their demands, family stress begins in earnest.

One of the hardest choices a single parent has to make is resisting change that offers improvement in order to protect the importance of maintenance. If the choice is made to go forward into change at the expense of maintenance, then this needs to be talked about with the children. The single parent has to explain the long-term gain, discuss the short-term costs, and devise strategies with the children to make those costs sufficiently bearable that stress does not become a harmful fact of all their daily lives.

12

~~~~~~

NOT GOING IT ALONE

CREATING A NETWORK OF SOCIAL SUPPORT

Two enemies of single parenthood are *fatigue* and *isolation*. Together they make any problem immeasurably worse. To lessen the likelihood of the fatigue, setting limits on demands and ensuring self-maintenance are important. To lessen isolation, the single parent needs social support.

Single parenthood is not a good excuse for being solitary: "I've gotten so used to living without another adult, I don't need any friends." And it is misplaced pride that boasts going it alone as a virtue: "I can handle everything by myself."

One of the first tasks of single parenthood is creating adequate social support. If as a consequence of divorce, for example, the extended family has been diminished and friends have allied with the former spouse, then this task becomes more difficult but no less important. If the single parent has never been a "joiner," then affiliating with a church, a self-help group, or a social activity may feel daunting, but it is worth the challenge. The more isolation the single parent chooses, the more vulnerable to stress and overreaction that person becomes.

Four kinds of support are needed, and part of each can be contributed by the children: sharing the care, emergency help, social companionship, and compassionate listening.

Sharing the care of children can partly be accomplished by training children to take more individual responsibility. A single parent can ask the question: "What am I routinely doing for my children that they can learn to do for themselves?" Then teach them. Education is preparation for independence. If the single parent is divorced and the ex-spouse is still cooperatively in the picture, then visitation provides a mechanism for sharing the care. Having people in other places who are happy to receive the children, like friends and neighbors, extended family and in-laws, creates security for children and provides relief for the single parent. This support allows for flexibility as plans change and unexpected needs inevitably arise. When a single parent has a community of friends, children become surrounded by a group of adults with whom they feel at home, and this social circle strengthens the children's sense of belonging and safety.

Emergency help needs to be discussed with children. Suppose they have a crisis and the single parent is not immediately available? Whom can they call? Where can they safely go? Both the single parent and the children need to know what these provisions are. Post a list of adult friends who have agreed to be available should there be a problem. Include addresses and phone numbers so children can immediately use the list if they have need.

Social companionship of children, no matter how enjoyable, is no substitute for the adult company of friends with whom the single parent can relate, independent of the parental role. Conversely, by becoming the major social friend for his or her children, the single parent can limit their desire for appropriate age companionship themselves. By setting an example of social independence, the single mother or father can encourage social independence in their children.

Because stressful times are inevitable for the single parent struggling to make ends meet, work problems out, and hold the family together, he or she needs someone to listen who will understand. And although it is important for children to be told when the parent is feeling upset and why (so they do not jump to false conclusions or wrongly implicate themselves), they should not serve in the role of major emotional confidante. If this occurs, the relationship becomes unhealthy. The roles start to reverse. Children begin assuming responsibility for the adult, with the primary care for their mother or father's emotional well-being coming to depend on them. They end up "parenting" their parent.

Compassionate listening from outside the family circle is important to the single parent because communicating about problems helps alleviate the stress. The single father or mother needs someone to call when the weight of responsibility, the uncertainty about what to do, or personal unhappiness creates emotional interference in the effective conduct of his or her life. This outside supporter does not need to be a problem solder, just a safe and caring person who, through nonjudgmental listening, will allow the single parent to express whatever perplexity, hurt, or frustration is being felt. Without the availability of someone with whom to *talk it out*, the single parent is at risk of emotionally closing off. Stuffed feelings and stored-up pain may then be *acted out*, most likely to the children's harm and the parent's later regret.

Support is like a combination safety net and safety valve. It allows the single parent to reach out and know he or she is not alone. It enables that parent to stay emotionally current with his or her experience, thereby reducing the likelihood of an unhappy overreaction when times get hard.

13

KEEPING PARENTING PERSPECTIVE

**RESPONDING TO PROBLEMS
WITHOUT OVERREACTING**

Parenting is an enormous responsibility. Just as they were shaped in their own family of origin, so single parents create the family of origin that will shape their child. The formative influences they provide, the behavior they model, the treatment they give, the guidance they offer, and the experience they allow will all affect their child's growth. When parenting alone, this responsibility can feel overwhelming.

Thus, the first task for single parents is to *relax*. They need to realize that they do not have to do everything "right" for their child to come out okay. Nobody parents "right." The best anyone can do is give a full faith effort, recognizing that the outcome depends on more than parenting alone. Significant additional factors include inborn characteristics of the child, outside events that influence the child, and choices by the child, over all of which parents have no direct control. Parenting is *not* responsible for everything that happens to the child or everything the child decides to do.

In addition, there is no universal parent capable of nurturing every potentiality that the child possesses. All parents are limited by who they are, by what they know, and by their past experience. More than this, the best they can provide the child is a mix, similar to the mix that their parents gave to them—of strength and frailty, of wisdom and stupidity, of wellness and illness, of consideration and insensitivity. And this, too, is okay. To be a parent is to be human, not perfect. The only way to be a perfect parent is to have a perfect child, and who would want to put a child under that kind of pressure?

It is best to allow the child imperfection, expecting him or her to create and encounter problems when impulse betrays, choice miscarries, or unforeseen difficulties arise. When single parents can keep this perspective, they don't overreact and make recovery from inevitable problems more difficult. To guard against overreacting, it helps to recognize statements commonly made when a parent "loses it" (perspective) in response to something in the child's life "gone wrong" (a problem).

Although parents are usually giving voice to frustration, what the child hears can feel like an indictment, another problem to add to the one he or she already has. A few of the more common overreactions to watch out for and avoid if possible are as follows:

- *"You'll never learn!"* No, the child just has not learned yet. Dooming the child's future is no help.
- *"You're nothing but a problem!"* No, a child is infinitely larger than the sum of his or her problems, and if the parent loses this perspective the child will too.
- *"You're only doing this to make me look bad!"* No, the child is usually too self-centered and shortsighted to consider how his or her actions affect the reputation of the parent.
- *"You're driving me crazy!"* No, the child is not responsible for the parent's state of mind. The parent is driving himself or herself crazy on behalf of the child.

47

- *"You're ruining the family!"* No, the child is not to blame for how the other members of the family are reacting. If the family is functioning badly, then everyone needs to own their part.

For a single parent, the burden of sole responsibility is felt most heavily when the child encounters problems. At such times, parental frustration and blaming are not helpful. Patience and perspective are what is needed. When a child makes a bad choice, that doesn't mean that he or she is a bad child, or that the parent is a bad parent.

When problems inevitably occur, parents need to hold fast to faith in themselves and their child, repeating to themselves and believing: "Good parents can have good children who sometimes make bad choices." Then parents need to go one step further. Every problem has a lesson to teach the child about himself or herself, about other people, and about life. Therefore, after the problem has been fixed, but before it is forgotten, the single parent needs to ask the child: "What have you learned from this experience that you didn't know before?"

14

~~~~~~

COMMUNICATION

KEEPING EVERYONE CONNECTED

Quality of family life depends as much as anything on quality of communication between the members. This is particularly true when adversity strikes or conflict arises. Then family relationships can become strained as the ability to effectively exchange information becomes tested by a sense of urgency or heightened emotionality. At times like these, what matters most is not so much what difficulties and differences the family goes through, as *how* they go through them. "How" has to do with the management of their communication with each other.

During periods of tension, there are many important communication questions that need to be affirmatively answered:

- In the face of family challenge, can members keep each other adequately informed?
- Can they remain securely connected?
- Can they express their authentic wants and needs?
- Can they listen to each other's concerns?
- Can they safely voice disagreements?
- Can they benefit from this continual exchange of information by deepening the bond of trust and intimacy between them?

Effective communication is the skill family members need to accomplish all these tasks, to answer all these questions.

To help maintain adequate communication, single parents have to model what they want. A nontalkative parent who complains about children who are inexpressive; a loud parent who yells at children to quiet down; a sarcastic parent who hates being ridiculed by children: all these parents are only modeling and encouraging behavior they are wanting to correct. Always, the first question parents must ask themselves when a child keeps misbehaving is a personal one: "Am *I* setting a poor example or otherwise enabling this misconduct myself?" If so, the most powerful way to help the child change his or her troublesome behavior is for parents to first change their own.

What is communication and why is it so important? A simple way to appreciate the power of communication is to think of it as an exchange of data about *feelings*, *thoughts*, and unobserved *behaviors*. Notice that unless a person shares this data about himself or herself, it remains private, accessible to other people only through guesswork and hearsay. Even among those who know us the best, even among family, *we are all strangers*. It takes sharing one's own data to become known, and listening to other people's data to understand them.

There is no mind reading. Each member of the family has two responsibilities. First, he or she must share personal data in order to be adequately known. Second, he or she must listen when others share to adequately understand. If family members stop doing either one of these basic communication behaviors, they become disconnected, insufficiently informed about each other's feelings, thoughts, and behaviors. For the single parent, being either a good sharer or a good listener is not enough. He or she must model both.

The power of communication becomes readily apparent when important data is insufficiently exchanged, when someone is not sharing or not listening enough. At this point, a significant psychological need within the family is violated—*the need to know*. Immediately, emotional costs are paid.

For example, consider the hypothetical case of Elisia, a single parent with two late-elementary-age children. Arriving home after work, she finds her son and daughter inexplicably missing. No message has been left to say where they have gone. Confronted with ignorance when she has an important need to know, Elisia becomes worried. Where are the children? After a half hour when there is still no word, her worry worsens. She becomes anxious. What if some harm has befallen them? After an additional hour of fruitless calls and helpless waiting, she begins to answer her dreadful questions with her own worst fears. Now she has begun projecting. Bad information feels better than no information at all, so she supplies it, finally concluding that the children must have gotten hurt on their way back from school. Then, in walk the children all smiles and giggles, happy to be home, happy to see her, but surprised to see a frown of disapproval on their mother's usually friendly face. Is something wrong, they wonder?

Does Elisia greet them with a cheerful "welcome home?" She does not. Instead, the children receive the brunt of her anger. "Where have you been and what do you mean running off without asking me first?"

Why the anger? When family members frustrate each other's need to know, resulting anxiety is often vented by blaming the person who chose not to share the missing information, in this case the children. "Don't you ever worry me like that again!" For the parent in this example, and for all family members in general, it is in everyone's best interests to keep each other adequately informed. This is one function of communication, to satisfy everyone's need to know.

Communication also serves another function, *creating self-definition through "speaking up."* Why is speaking up important? Because it allows each family member to satisfy a second psychological need—*the need to be known.* This function of communication is fulfilled in a variety of important ways:

- Speaking up lets a person *express* thoughts and feelings through sharing his or her experience.
- Speaking up lets a person *explain* opinions and beliefs in order to declare his or her view.
- Speaking up lets a person *question* in order to understand what is happening, asking to find out.
- Speaking up lets a person *confront* unacceptable treatment by taking stands when he or she feels wronged.
- Speaking up lets a person *resolve* disagreements through contesting differences with others.

Through all five ways of speaking up, each member honors his or her *responsibility for being known* by others in the family. In the process he or she becomes publicly *defined* as an individual. For a child to learn how to speak up in a family, single parents must ensure that three conditions are in place:

1. Single parents must *model* speaking up themselves.
2. They must *value* speaking up when the children do it.
3. They must create a family environment in which speaking up feels *safe* from any threat of injury or reprisal.

The legacy of learning to speak up in one's family of origin is that children will feel comfortable being *socially outspoken* in their peer and later adult relationships. They will be empowered to use communication to assert their needs and wants, and to defend their limits. Unhappily, the opposite legacy may afflict those children who grow up in a family where speaking up is not modeled, valued, or safe. They acquire a different set of skills: *shutting up*. Instead of learning to express their inner experience, they learn to remain *silent*. Instead of learning to declare their views, they learn to *defer* to the views of others. Instead of learning to question to find out, they learn to *wait* to be told. Instead of learning to assert themselves against unacceptable treatment, they learn to *accept* any treatment given. Instead of learning to contest significant differences, they learn to *concede* to avoid conflict. In consequence of this education in shutting up, children can grow up becoming *socially compliant* to their cost. They are in danger of living too much on other people's terms and not enough on their own. They are in danger of denying self-definition from a reluctance to speak up. In the extreme, they are at risk of becoming victims in later relationships.

Certainly speaking up needs to have limits, as when it keeps others from having their say. After all, one positive form of shutting up is listening, and children need to learn how to do that too. Speaking up needs to be done in a nonabusive, nonhurtful manner as well. To these ends, single parents should model the manner of speech they want children to learn, and monitor family communication to keep it within bounds of consideration and respect. To remain adequately connected and sufficiently defined, however, each family member must be given the freedom, and take the responsibility, for speaking up on his or her own behalf. The need to know and the need to be known are at stake.

15

▲▲▲

AUTHORITY

ASSERTING INFLUENCE TO GAIN CONTROL

A family system is defined by the values of the parents. Mothers and fathers are responsible for establishing beliefs, setting norms, and making rules for themselves and their children to live by. When the loss of a spouse occurs, the single mother or father reclarifies those family values now that he or she is parenting alone. Some old values that were associated with the former spouse may be set aside, whereas some new values may need to be installed to make the reconstituted family work. The departed partner's emphasis on following orders and no talking back, for example, may be relaxed by the single parent who is now more concerned with getting children to think for themselves and to feel safe speaking up.

A child learns parental values by instruction, by example, and from stands the father or mother takes by exercising *authority.* If after requesting, reasoning, and explaining what should or should not occur, a parent still finds that the child is reluctant to conform (to fit in) or comply (to go along), then authority may need to be asserted. There are five common forms of social authority upon which parents tend to rely:

1. Making demands
2. Setting limits
3. Asking questions
4. Confronting to discuss
5. Applying consequences

Asserting authority does not usually earn parents immediate favor in their son's or daughter's eyes. A willful or adolescent child can respond with considerable displeasure when being told what can't happen or what must be done. For single parents, with no co-parent to back them up, asserting authority can require courage. They must act for their own, the family's, or the child's well being against what the child may strongly desire. The child doesn't like being denied, the parent doesn't like being disliked. Assuming they are not threatening or abusive in their exercise of power, however, parents need to stand by the values they believe in, insisting on the conformity and compliance they need. Although children may resent this imposition of authority at the moment, and treat the parent more as an enemy than a friend, over time a firm and well-intentioned authority conveys love, creates security, and engenders respect. The parent cares enough to oppose the children's wants for the sake of their best interests.

Because a child's behavior ultimately depends on his or her own decisions, parents do not have actual control over their son or daughter. Compliance and conformity mean that the child has *chosen to cooperate* by giving *consent* to what parents want or do not want to have happen. The early adolescent child who defiantly declares, "You can't make me and you can't stop me!" *is* telling the truth. Fortunately, to be without absolute control does not mean parents are without influence. They can encourage the child's consent to go along with their authority in four significant ways. They can use their powers of *guidance, supervision*, and *structure*, and they can work the *exchange points*.

Guidance is the power of persuasion. Here the parent *explains* what is wanted and why. More than that, guidance means providing children with a stream of feedback about their conduct, a running commentary on which of their decisions are working well, and which are not. Persistent parents never shut up. They explain, they evaluate, and they editorialize to keep the child aware of their caring point of view. When the child doesn't want to hear, appears not to listen, or refuses to act upon what he or she has been told, persistent parents don't get discouraged. They keep on talking. Why? Because they know that part of their job is to provide a continuing source of reference on which the child can rely and trust. Although parents may not always listen to their child, the child listens to the parents. The child enters everything they say, receiving and remembering what they've been told, secure in knowing what those parents think and where they stand. *Good parents are relentless communicators.*

Supervision is the power of pursuit. Here parents commit to keeping after the child to take care of business at home, at school, and out in the world. Supervision is *nagging*, and nagging is honorable work. It needs to be done. Unhappily, it is also the drudge work of parenting. The child doesn't like receiving it, and parents don't like doing it. Nagging essentially says: "I will keep after you and after you and after you until you finally get what I wanted done." It wears the child's resistance down. Children know it works because when they want something that is initially refused, they will nag and nag and nag to see if they can wear the parent down into giving up and giving in, and sometimes they can. Through this exhausting repetition, parents show that they will use the power of their insistence to overcome the child's resistance—to get a chore at last accomplished, to get homework finally done. *Good parents are persistent naggers.*

Structure is the power of punishment. Reserved for major rule violations (not resisting chores, which calls for supervision), structure describes the boundaries of allowable behavior. When children breach those boundaries, consequences (punishments) are applied. Sometimes *natural consequences* can occur. For example, when a child uses what has been forbidden only to get hurt, the resulting injury teaches more powerfully than parental punishment could instruct. Other times, however, parents must devise adverse consequences where no natural ones exist. These consequences can catch the children's attention, thereby causing them to rethink what they have done, and encourage them back into the range of acceptable conduct.

The three kinds of consequences most commonly applied are *physical hurt, deprivation,* and *reparation.* Of these, physical hurt—deliberately inflicting pain—is the most problematic. With very young children it may instill fear of the much larger parent, instead of respect. With older children it may arouse resentment from the humiliation of being "beaten." Adolescents who receive this kind of correction often describe their parent with the contempt reserved for a bully whose power just depends on superior strength and size. The danger of physical punishment is in the other learnings it may teach: "Might is right" and "Compliance is best secured not by reason, but by force." In the worst case, when anger carries physical punishment to extremes—parents spanking, whipping, or hitting to relieve personal frustration or to show the child "Who's Boss,"—the lesson learned is not caring correction, but abuse.

Deprivation—restricting the child's freedom of movement or use—is most effective when applied short-term. A time-out for a younger child or an evening's grounding for an adolescent provides a period to reconsider actions and to resolve not to repeat the same offense. When parents totally strip a child, however, curtailing every valued freedom and privilege for a long duration, they can end up empowering their errant son or daughter because now he or she has nothing left to lose. Not only that, they haven't actually asked the child to do anything, only to do without. Passive adjustments may be unpleasant, but they are undemanding. In addition, by ordering the child confined to the premises with no use of the telephone or the television, parents must grudgingly stay home to make sure that their sanctions are obeyed. Who has been grounded now?

Probably the most effective punishment of all is *reparation*. Using this approach the parent declares: "As a consequence of breaking the rule, you shall have to work the violation off. Before whatever else you want to do, this task must first be completed to my satisfaction." Working off the offense causes children to do something around the home the parent would like to get done, in the process paying for their "crime." Reparation is a constructive punishment because the child is required to make some active contribution. The reason why many parents resist using reparation is that it requires more supervision than deprivation. Because it is the most arduous consequence to apply, however, reparation also reinforces the most parental authority. *Good parents keep punishment constructive.*

Working the *exchange points* exploits the child's dependency on parents for various permissions, services, and resources they control. What the parent essentially says to the noncooperative child is this: "Before you can have what you want from me, I want to get what I want from you—the chore I asked you to accomplish." Here the parent is invoking the principle of exchange. The child is being told that to receive benefits from the family, he or she has to contribute to the family as well. Unless this principle of exchange has been enforced, a child may become more inclined to take from the parent than give. Soon the parent will begin feeling exploited and grow resentful: "I am giving so much and getting so little in return!" Thus, when a child starts refusing to perform routine household responsibilities, parents can delay what they would normally provide. They would be happy to drive the child over to a friend's, for example, but only *after* the trash has been taken out. A working parent/child relationship requires giving on *both* sides, not just one. If a parent grows tired of asking and nagging and still not getting a chore done, wait for the next exchange point. Sooner or later the child shall want some parental service, provision, or permission. Then withhold what the child wants until you get what you want. If promises are made by the child to do it later, after getting what he or she desires, explain that because such promises have not been kept in the past, they have become false currency. From now on, performance is what counts. *After* the child performs for the parent, the parent will perform for the child. *Good parents insist on an adequate exchange.*

To assert authority does not mean parents have to become harshly authoritarian, only that they must be willing to back up the beliefs they hold and the needs they have by the stands they take. They don't have to arouse fear or inflict harm, but they do need to be willing to put their popularity at risk, sometimes sacrificing being liked now for being respected later.

16

▲▲

RESPONSIBILITY

PREPARING FOR SELF-SUFFICIENCY

Infants are born into a state of dependency, gradually learning independence as they grow up, until by the time they reach *trial independence* (roughly between the ages of eighteen and twenty-three) they are ready to try living on their own. *Responsibility* is the power of self-sufficiency. It is not innate; it must be learned. This is why so much of parenting is preparation with this end in mind.

But what responsibilities should a parent teach a child and when? To answer this question, single parents can ask themselves another: "At the end of adolescence, what exit skills, exposures to experience, and understandings for taking care of themselves do I want my children to have learned?" After listing these requirements for independent living, single parents can ask a further question: "At what age do I want to start teaching which of these responsibilities?"

Preparation for responsibility can be planned. When to begin instruction in what responsibility will vary depending on the child's age and parental assessment of readiness to acquire that self-sufficiency. Responsibility for picking up one's belongings is usually taught before graduating to household chores. Responsibility for finding one's way around the neighborhood is usually assigned before mastering public transportation to get around town, and so on.

The problem with teaching responsibility is that it usually requires putting the child at risk. After providing instruction, example, and guided and independent practice, parents must finally give freedom and leave the child at the mercy of his or her own decision making, for good or ill. They must release control over that part of the child's life. This letting go is the hardest part of parenting. These decisions can be agonizing because consequences from something going wrong can be so costly, leaving the child hurt and the parents ridden with guilt. When to leave a child unattended at home? When to let an elementary school child walk alone to school? When to let an older child begin to date, to drive, or to start a part-time job? There are no guarantees that the child is ready. There is only assessing how well the child is managing the rest of his or her life, and using *constructive worry* to anticipate the unexpected.

Parental worry is constructive when it asks "What if?" causing the child to consider risks attendant upon the freedom he or she is wanting. "That's not going to happen to me, I wish you'd stop worrying!" objects the child, impatient to get going. The parent answers: "I'm not saying it will happen to you, only that it could. Therefore, before I let you go, we are going to talk about how you would cope if such a consequence did occur." Contingency planning is one protection parents can provide. Constructive worry can pose questions a child, eager for freedom, will not think to ask. Constructive worry can assess the unknowns in a situation. Constructive worry can teach children to think ahead.

What if the child does choose unwisely and encounters difficulty? What should parents do? Should they rescue the child and never allow any further freedoms? No. Growing into responsibility inevitably entails risk. No matter how well prepared, undertaking what one has not done before usually requires some learning of the trial and error kind. Having chosen foolishly, the child must be held accountable for the decisions he or she has made. Figuring out how to recover from painful consequences helps the child learn to better handle that situation responsibly the next time it arises. After all, the child doesn't want to experience that pain again.

Then there are mishaps that occur as no obvious consequence of the child's choice. "I was just driving down the street and this guy runs a stop sign and hits me." *Just because one was not "at fault," accidents are not allowed as excuses to escape all responsibility.* What was the child thinking about when choosing to be in the wrong place at the wrong time? "I was in a hurry and wanted to take a short-cut home." Was there anything the child could have done differently in that situation that might have averted the problem? "I could have checked the side streets more carefully for oncoming traffic." The best insurance against repeating a bad choice later is learning from a bad choice now. There are two major safeguards for children growing up. The self-protection parents can influence is responsibility. The one they cannot is luck. Given this reality, they should support development of all the responsibility they can.

Because single parenting is so demanding, training children to early responsibility becomes important. Teaching children to operate independently at home by becoming self-regulated eases the single parent's load. Deciding when to shift this load of responsibility depends on the parent answering two questions:

1. The *provision question* is: "What am I doing for my children that they could learn to do for themselves?"
2. The *protection question* is: "What am I keeping my children from doing that they could safely learn to do for themselves?"

Teaching responsibility trains children to become more independent through learning to help out. It is also a preparation for adulthood, each step along the way enhancing children's esteem as they feel more competent to take care of themselves.

17

HONESTY

THE NEED FOR SPEAKING THE TRUTH

Trust, intimacy, safety: for these to thrive in families the *truth* must be told. Deny or lie about the truth, and communication—that lifeline of sharing data that keeps members confidently connected—is immediately threatened. Distrust is aroused, anxiety builds, insecurity is experienced, hurt is given, offense is taken, and distance is felt.

Good decisions depend on valid data. Parenting is a constant process of decision making that depends heavily on data the child discloses. Misinformed, parents can give permission when they should say "no." They can assume all is well when all is not. They can even ignore warning signs, having been falsely assured that parental fears are rooted in imagination. "Come on, be serious! Me use drugs? You've got to be kidding. You know me better than that!" But how can parents know their child if they are not told the truth?

The problem is, children find many motivations to lie:

- They lie to deny painful reality.
- They lie to compensate for feeling bad about themselves.
- They lie to outsmart authorities.
- They lie to cover up wrongdoing to escape from being caught.
- They lie to be allowed to do what has expressly been forbidden.

Lying is an act of power, with the child creating false impressions to manipulate the adult world. Because it can be so damaging, parents must confront the child when he or she shows evidence of lying. They must let the child know how it feels to be lied to, apply consequences if they so choose, and finally reinstate trust that has been injured, lost, or broken. This reinstatement is hard to do when the initial tendency after being lied to may sound something like this: "Trust you? Not anytime soon. You're going to have to earn it back!"

Maintaining a stance of distrust, however, is not functional for the parent or the child. Parents will drive themselves to distraction with suspicion while the child may give up on telling the truth. Having been told that parental trust has been totally lost, the child figures there's no longer any point in telling the truth since even honesty will now be disbelieved. For the sake of both the parent and the child, trust must be extended once more. The mother or father must resolve to act on trust, ready to call the child again on any further lying, should it occur.

As the child grows into adolescence, telling the truth becomes more hotly contested. With the teenager urgently wanting more freedom out in the world, parents have an increased need to know at a time when many young people have a decreased willingness to tell. Given what they want to do, many teenagers rightly conclude that telling the truth to a parent may not set them free. All children grow up partly within, and partly outside, the rules set by their parents. Consequently, when they knowingly violate those rules, they are tempted to distort or deny the truth.

At this juncture, parents need to make the contract between them and their adolescent absolutely clear. If they are going to risk giving the teenager the freedom he or she wants, then the teenager must provide them with adequate and trustworthy information, as well as responsible conduct out in the world.

During adolescence, some teenagers will repeatedly exploit parental ignorance by lying in order to get illicit freedom that is desired or to escape certain punishment that is deserved. Because parents often do not have sufficient evidence of lying to be absolutely sure, and because the most common teenage defense against lying is denial, the guidelines for dealing with *suspected lying* are difficult but necessary to follow.

1. Check out other sources of information.
2. Repeatedly question the teenager's story for any inconsistencies.
3. Assess the teenager's range of social experience for possible activities he or she might want to cover up.
4. Feel if the teenager is keeping more distance and has become less communicative in the family.
5. If parents are more sure than not that lying has occurred, confront the teenager as though lying is the truth.

Because direct proof can be so hard to come by, reasonable doubt has to be enough. This means that when doubt turns out to be unfounded, and the charge proves false, the teenager feels unfairly accused. In this case, damage to the relationship results. The teenager can feel legitimately hurt. "How could you believe I would do such a thing? My own parent! How could you?" Then the parent has to explain the evidence and chain of reasoning that led to this false conclusion, and apologize for being wrong. Teenage lying is one of those hard problems with very hard solutions. It is risky to abide, and it is risky to confront.

As a preventive, however, when a child enters adolescence, single parents can usefully share some information with the teenager about the high costs of lying. Although they understand that no teenager will tell all the truth about everything going on in his or her increasingly independent life, they can still itemize some of the damage lying can do.

1. *Liars injure those they love.* Being told a lie can cause parents to feel hurt from lack of respect, anger from betrayal of trust, and fear from loss of control.

2. *Liars are doubly punished.* They are penalized both for the offense and for the untruth they told.

3. *Liars complicate their lives.* In leading a double life, they must keep track of the truth about what happened, the fiction they have told, and remember the difference between them.

4. *Liars live in fear of being found out.* By keeping the truth secret with dishonesty, liars keep their lives feeling unsafe.

5. *Liars feel out of control.* Lies beget more lies. To cover up one lie, children feel they must make up another, creating more unreality than they can manage. Soon they lose track of all the lies they've told.

6. *Liars are lonely people.* Pulling away and becoming distant to keep truth from being discovered, they become isolated by avoiding contact, particularly with those they love.

7. *Liars lower their self-esteem.* Liars mistreat themselves every time they lie by admitting lack of capacity, confidence, or courage to deal directly with whatever reality they are trying to conceal.

8. *Liars can fool themselves.* To make themselves feel better, they may actually convince themselves that the lies they told were true. They can lie to themselves.

9. *Liars feel guilty.* Knowing they have abused the trust of those they love, they can come to feel badly on that account.

10. *Liars live in a hostile world.* The more people they lie to, the more anger and distrust they reap in return.

11. *Liars are relieved to be found out.* Honesty relaxes relationships by restoring trust and closeness once again. Now there is no longer any need to live in hiding.

12. *Liars discover the truth about lying.* It is far less stressful to be the person lied to than the person who must live by telling lies.

For all these reasons, when the child is living in a world of deceit that his or her own lying has created, the single parent can offer a sympathetic way out. The mother or father can say something like this: "It's hard to lie to those you love without feeling pressure. To relieve your pressure, I'd like you to know I know you have been lying. When you want to talk about it and get back on an honest footing with me again, please let me know."

18

MUTUALITY

RESPECTING ONESELF AND OTHERS

People, children included, are creatures of habit. Habit is created through repetition. Learned patterns of behavior become increasingly automatic and hard to break the more they are practiced. Parents, by setting examples and limits, by giving instructions and making demands, help shape the daily living habits of their child. Among the habits that are learned at home are those about how to act in relationship to others.

Keeping children "nice" to live with requires parental training in *mutuality*. Mutuality means keeping some equitable balance between striving to satisfy the needs of oneself and the needs of others. Somewhere between the extremes of total denial of self (subservience to others) and total indulgence of self (exploitation of others) is a middle way where the needs of self and others in relationships are both respected. Learning this definition is important for children both now and later. If mutuality is learned when children are young, then they carry this interpersonal habit into significant partnerships when they are older. If not, they are at risk of acting so self-sacrificing or so self-centering it will be to the cost of those later relationships. How the child is taught to act now is how the adult comes to behave later.

What is mutuality? It is three codes of conduct combined into one. It is reciprocity, compromise, and sensitivity.

Reciprocity

The first of these, *reciprocity*, means learning to maintain a working *exchange* so that giving and receiving benefits in the parent/child relationship goes two ways. The parent gives *and* the child gives in return. Sometimes single parents can become so preoccupied with satisfying what their child wants, particularly after the pain of parental death or divorce, that they focus exclusively on the child's well-being, setting their own aside. Neglecting to insist that the child still do for them, reciprocity is lost. Soon they find themselves catering to a selfish child who knows no better than to act like the only needs and interests that matter are his or her own. What a shame for a child to be taught to act so "spoiled." The moral is: *Selfless parents are at risk of raising selfish children.*

Compromise

Compromise is the willingness to seek a *middle ground* when a difference in wants occur. Each party consents to move off his or her own immediate self-interest in order to construct a common resolution partially responsive to the needs of both. Children need help learning this principle of compromise. In order to get some of their way, they have to give up some of their way. Most important, they must accept that *some is enough*. They don't have to settle differences either by having it all or making due with nothing. "It's either going to have to be my way, your way, or no way!" Extremes are not the best answer. Compromise says: "Let's find *our* way, where each of us gets some of what we want."

Compromise can be hard to teach, particularly during adolescence, when a teenager becomes extremely urgent about expressing wants. He or she may demand it *all* and demand it *now*. Under this kind of pressure, single parents need to give a *moderate* response, teaching the child to compromise on how much want is satisfied and when it is delivered, diluting and delaying gratification. If single parents can't take stands for compromise and moderation, then the child just keeps pushing for complete and immediate fulfillment. Desires are treated as demands, and demands as entitlements. The moral is: *Parents who want to give everything to make their son or daughter happy, risk raising a child who is only happy when he or she is given everything that is desired.*

Sensitivity

In families, members demonstrate *sensitivity* by showing *consideration* for each other's emotional well-being. They do not knowingly act in ways that are painful to anyone else. Because of family intimacy, members come to know each other very well. They become familiar with one another's insecurities, weaknesses, and sore points, and with one another's sources of regret and guilt and shame. Single parents need to take a stand for sensitivity. Attacking other members where they hurt in order to get one's way, to get even, or to poke harmful fun is not allowed. Teasing that torments, criticism that injures, and sarcasm that humiliates are not only insensitive, they can be abusive. The moral is: *Parents who don't take stands for sensitivity are at risk of raising children who believe ignoring or attacking the vulnerabilities of others is okay.*

A child who has not been taught the lessons of mutuality is a difficult child to live with now and a difficult adult to live with later on. Parenting is preparation because it shapes future behavior. Single parents and their children are best served when mutuality is a founding principle of family life.

19

~~~~~~

THE ONLY CHILD

HIGH-PRESSURE PARENTING

Sometimes parents, feeling overrun by the demands of multiple children and their many conflicts, will long for a simpler family system. "Oh how much easier it would have been to have had a single child!" This is not necessarily so. Having an only child is high-pressure parenting. Their son or daughter is the first and the last child in one—the only chance for parenting they get—so they want to do it right.

Parental preoccupation and attachment to their child is increased when the son or daughter is the only child they have. The relationship becomes extremely sensitized, with parents and child highly attuned to each other. Closeness causes them each to become very concerned with pleasing, with making sure the other feels okay. Frequently one will register emotional distress when the other is troubled or upset.

In this intensified relationship, it is easy for expectations of conduct and achievement to become exaggerated. Parents sincerely want to give the child their best, whereas the child feels an enormous obligation to do his or her best in return. Bonding becomes extremely tight. Thriving under undiluted parental attention, the child comes to treat parents as the most important people in his or her world, and enjoys being treated as most important by them.

Because the triad of two parents and an only child makes such a tight family unit, when divorce divides the family in two, the child has a lot to lose. Destroyed is the family world that revolved around the child. There is now one less parent in residence to meet his or her needs. Because the remaining single parent is busier and, therefore, less available, he or she delays and denies more requests by the child that were automatically gratified before. The only child must adjust to some parental responses that feel new and disagreeable. "Not now." "I have other things I need to do." "Maybe later." "No, you can't." For many only children, divorce takes a lot of getting used to.

For the only child of divorce, seeing either parent can be painful because when with one, he or she misses the other. The child longs for the old cozy threesome they once made. This pain becomes immeasurably worse if divorced parents can't let go of grievances against each other. Their ongoing antagonism divides the child's loyalty, causing him or her to experience deep inner conflict. So close to each, loving them both so much, whose side should the child take? The greatest blessing that divorcing parents can give their only child is to make peace with each other as soon as they honestly can. Remember, only children take parental divorce extremely hard.

Beyond the impact of divorce, however, are some common traits most only children share that can occasionally become cause for concern. These traits are learned as a function of being the only child in a family. They have to do with self-definition, socialization, standards, sharing, and separation.

Self-definition

Most only children are very well *self-defined* (and this includes first children, who are only children for awhile). They tend to be encouraged to express and develop themselves because their interests and potentials are so closely noticed and well nurtured at home. Their efforts are encouraged and their achievements are rewarded. Recipients of so much parental attention and support, they can develop an exaggerated sense of self-assurance and self-importance. Full of themselves, only children can act in their relationships like they count more than anybody else. Should this occur, only children may need help respecting the valid needs of others.

Socialization

Because there are no other children in the family, the only child tends to spend time with who is there—his or her parents. Primarily *socialized* to older companionship and conversation, the only child identifies with these significant adults. Becoming used to interacting with parents and their social circle for company, an only child can learn to get on better with adults than with peers. For this reason, he or she may need help reaching out and making friends with children the same age. Being frequently complimented for acting grown up, an only child can precociously acquire the skills of acting older. He or she may learn to treat adults as equals, not easily deferring to their authority. Should these consequences occur, the only child may need help learning to question less and to comply more readily with outside authorities, like teachers at school.

Standards

By placing themselves on equal standing with their parents, only children come to presume adult equivalence. In the process, they often apply to themselves equal *standards* of competence and achievement. However, they are not adults. They are children, so these self-imposed adult expectations for performance just create unrealistic pressure to measure up. A common outcome of this pressure is the development of characteristics very difficult for only children to endure. These include becoming easily frustrated, perfectionistic, impatient, self-critical, and extremely hard on themselves when they fall short of goals, make mistakes, or fail. Should these stresses begin to afflict the only child, he or she may need help resetting standards appropriate for his or her own age.

Sharing

Used to playing by themselves and not with other siblings, only children may have a hard time learning how to *share* with a peer. Because so much of what they do for fun is done on their own terms, they can enter friendship with a sense of entitlement when it comes to play. "Let's do what I want." "Let's do it my way." In consequence, peers may socially reject them for being too controlling and judgmental to be fun. This is why many only children prefer socializing with a younger friend. That way they can choose the focus and set the rules of play. Should this isolation or dominance occur, the only child may need help learning to share for the sake of companionship.

Separation

Finally, because the bonding with parents is so close, *separation* can be difficult. Leaving childhood for adolescence can be delayed because only children are reluctant to push against and pull away from parents for independence. It can feel scary to create distance from those with whom they are so powerfully connected. Adolescence is a process of separation. For only children, this growing apart can be extremely threatening when they are so emotionally tied and socially dependent on their parents. Leaving home at the end of adolescence can also be a hard separation, releasing the security of family. Should the letting go prove difficult, either at the beginning or end of adolescence, only children may need to be encouraged into social independence by their parents.

20

THE GOOD CHILD
AND THE BAD

WHEN ONE CHILD COMPLIES
AND THE OTHER DOESN'T

L ike most other kinds of human systems, families are held together by social authority asserted from above and social consent given from below. Parents are supposed to provide that authority by setting norms and rules, and children are expected to obey, conforming to those norms by fitting in, and complying with those rules by going along.

If every child conformed and complied all the time, then parents would have an easy time of parenting. However, such is not the case, particularly when there are multiple children in a family, each wanting room to be his or her own individual person.

Thus, if Child Number One, the only child for awhile, fulfills most every wish and requirement that parents have, he or she may stake such a strong claim to their approval that Child Number Two feels unable to compete, gives up, and decides to self-define another way. Refusing to be a copy of Number One, Child Number Two decides to claim individuality by asserting differentness, setting himself or herself apart from the rest of the family no matter what the costs.

Opposition often becomes the chosen path to follow when it feels as if approval has been denied. In this case, Child

Number Two conforms less well to family norms, thereby stressing the limits of parental tolerance, and complies less readily, thereby pushing the limits of parental patience. Initially accustomed to the ease of parenting Child Number One, parents find Number Two much more demanding and less rewarding to raise. "Our hard child" is how they come to describe Number Two, wondering what is wrong with him or her, sometimes growing tired of dealing with the constant difficulty. At their most exhausted, they may even blame the hard child for not being as easy as the other son or daughter.

Comparison is the enemy of acceptance. When parents judge one child easy and another hard, they are beginning a chain of evaluation that can lead them into equating easy with "good" and hard with "bad." From this distinction an appearance of favoritism can arise, the easy child receiving more positive attention, the hard child receiving more of the negative. Feeling rejected by this implied preference and unfair treatment, the bad child may act out in anger, thereby increasing his or her "bad" family reputation. Although the easy child keeps getting appreciated and rewarded, the hard child keeps getting disapproved of and punished. The hard child becomes a lightning rod for family conflict, whereas the easy child is a constant source of credit to the parents.

Because heading a single parent family can be so demanding, a mother or father's needs for conformity and compliance can become increased by the need to keep everything running as smoothly as possible. Given all there is now to manage, single parents may not look kindly on an obstructive or disruptive child. To make the family function, single parents must be given sufficient cooperation. When they are not, however, they must avoid the good child/bad child distinction, because the consequences can be extremely damaging.

Once this comparison is fixed in the mind of the parent and in the hearts of the children, dehumanizing forces are set in motion. The good child may become determined to live on best behavior, fearing anything less might injure reputation in the family. He or she dreads resembling the bad child and being treated accordingly by the parent. As for the bad child, he or she may become even more determined to live on worst behavior. Having given up the possibility of ever pleasing or succeeding, the bad child may resolve to live defiantly on his or her own angry terms.

Then, a mutual resentment builds between the two children. The bad child sees the good one as the family favorite, being better treated and better loved. The good child sees the bad sibling as the family focus, claiming much more parental attention, and being unfairly given special allowances and second chances for doing wrong. Envy of each other fuels the conflict between them.

Come the end of adolescence, however, it is usually the bad child, and not the good one, who is better situated to claim a happy independence. "Bad" children can honestly say that their single parent has known them at their worst, can apologize and make amends, then place that relationship back on a positive footing and go forward ready to change their ways. "Good" children, however, are often placed in a much harder predicament. They have become so wed to an image of goodness that doing even the slightest wrong feels disallowed. To be less than perfect threatens to lose them not only approval, but maybe even love. Feeling denied permission for being less than pleasing, good children can continue to be burdened by resentment on this account.

The truth is, every child needs freedom to be both good and bad, to express and integrate their positive and negative sides. Therefore, to the extremely good child it may be helpful to explain: "Everybody sometimes misbehaves, and that's okay. I'm certainly not perfect all the time. But you keep loving me when I mess up, and that is just the way I would keep on loving you." As to the child who seems to thrive on being bad, a parent can appreciate the positive when it occurs and affirm the good. "Getting into trouble is *not* all you do. There is much that I love and appreciate about how you conduct your life, and I want to tell you what that is."

21

SIBLING CONFLICT

WHY CHILDREN FIGHT AND WHAT TO DO ABOUT IT

For many parents, conflict is a stressor. It arouses frustration from opposition, anger from frustration, and perhaps hurt from anger. Parents dislike fighting with their children because it is fatiguing and injects negativity into the relationship. However, even more wearing than fighting between parents and child, is what appears to be the never-ending conflict between children. Why can't they just leave each other alone?

Sibling conflict, although an irritant for the parents, serves the growth needs of children by allowing them to ventilate emotion, vie for power, and defend differences between them. When parents cite the constant fighting as evidence that their children just can't get along, this is a misperception. *Fighting is how they get along.*

Certain factors tend to increase the frequency of conflict. If the siblings are close in age or if they are the same sex, competition to establish dominance and differentness becomes ongoing. Thus, the older puts the younger rival down to maintain supremacy, whereas the younger asserts power by provoking the older into paying attention to him or her. The older teases to demonstrate verbal superiority, the younger imitates to imply offensive equality. "He's teasing me!" "She's copying me!" are testimony to the power of these tactics to provoke a fight. In the memorable words of one ten-year-old: "Fighting can be fun. I get to make my brother feel mad, bad, and sad."

In the short-term, loss of one parent in the home can increase sibling conflict as children act out their hurt and anger by fighting with each other. They also compete for what is now a scarce resource, the single parent's attention. "Sometimes they seem to get along better when I'm not around," single parents will observe. Often they are correct. Remove the object of the contest and the contest is suspended, until the single parent returns.

How can the single parent moderate this conflict?

1. *Hold both children responsible for any conflict that occurs.* Do not be manipulated into taking sides. Conflict is cooperative. "Suppose they gave a war and nobody came?" or only one person came? It takes two to create a fight, but only one to stop it.
2. *Do not try to figure out who started it.* They both did. Asking who started it will only elicit a chain of blame, arguing back and forth about who first did this to cause the other to do that.
3. *Don't arbitrate, separate.* Usually the single parent's settlement will be resented because the children consider it insufficient or unjust. "Blessed be the arbitrator for they shall be hated by both sides." Let them figure out how to resolve their differences, at most helping mediate the communication when they get stuck.
4. *Do allow tattling to the parent.* Encourage both children to come to the parent when fighting seems to be getting out of hand. Sometimes conflict will escalate beyond the children's capacity to keep from doing each other harm. Then, the single parent has a role to act as *governor*, intervening to stop the fighting and separate the combatants for safety's sake.

5. *Do monitor the conduct of the conflict for abuse.* Although the single parent holds both children cooperatively responsible for creating the conflict, he or she must hold them each separately accountable for their conduct in the conflict.

6. The rule of safety must always apply: *In families, conflict is never an excuse for inflicting injury on another person.* "I only did that, I only said that, because I was angry" is no excuse. The child needs to find a nondestructive way to manage his or her anger. For a single parent to permit doing injury in sibling conflict, whether physical or emotional, is to endorse abuse. One child learns it is okay to do deliberate harm when fighting, whereas the other finds out that it is acceptable to receive that kind of treatment from another family member. If these lessons are learned in childhood, they often are applied to adult relationships later on.

Assuming fighting is kept within the bounds of safety, sibling conflict is healthy and to be expected. The older child, often the larger, must learn restraint when fighting with the younger, whereas the younger, often the smaller, must learn courage to stand ground against the older. As for single parents, when they can no longer stand the bickering and arguing and tussling, they can declare a separation for their own sake. Although often not stressful for the children, their conflict becomes wearing to the parent who decides he or she has had enough for the moment and is entitled to some relief: "Go to your rooms!"

22

~~~~~~

THE ABSENT FATHER

COMPENSATING FOR THE MISSING PARENT

Part of the power of parents is the presence they provide, giving children adult models to interact with and follow as they grow. Sex role definition is learned from the presence of both parents. What a boy learns to believe about being a man and how to behave as a man depends on identifying with his father and adjusting to his mother's treatment of her son's masculinity. Conversely, what a girl learns to believe about being a woman and how to behave as a woman depends on identifying with her mother and adjusting to her father's treatment of his daughter's femininity.

This part of their development becomes increasingly important once children begin to separate from childhood and enter adolescence (roughly between the ages of nine and thirteen) in search of social independence from the family. Now they become curious to begin experimenting and experiencing themselves in more adult ways. At this point in the adolescent's life, a lot of powerful sex role models begin competing for the child's loyalty. There are idealized images of men and women in commercial advertising. There are cultural heroes and heroines from the world of sports and entertainment. And there are the popular kids at school who embody the most socially approved peer group stereotypes that other children, to gain acceptance, strive to fit.

At this age, these competing images, models, and stereotypes tend to be restrictive (male = be tough and don't show hurt; female = be sweet and don't show anger); they can be harmful (male = controlling; female = compliant); and they are often exploitive (male = supposed to take; female = supposed to give). To offset the limiting and negative influences their children's peer and popular culture have to offer, parents must provide alternative and more complete sex role definitions.

When a single parent is all the parental presence there is, *and in the vast majority of instances the single parent is the mother*, the effects of the absent parent, in this case the father, must be addressed. Sons or daughters growing up with little or no contact with their fathers are at risk of some damaging effects.

In the absence of a father to provide the primary male model and male response, adolescent children become more susceptible to the competing models idealized by peers and popular culture. Thus, an adolescent son without a father may come to rely on other teenage boys to example appropriate male definition. Adopting their manly posturing in order to be accepted by this group, he comes to identify with a set of immature stereotypes that may include using girls sexually to prove his masculinity. Meanwhile, an adolescent daughter without a father may turn to opposite sex peers to provide the missing model, to provide primary male attachment. She may accept their stereotypical treatment of females in order to fulfill her need for a significant male relationship, even if that relationship is conducted on exploitive terms.

The single-parent mother, without a father present, has the power to counter these negative sex role influences. How she treats her son as a man has formative effect (male = responsible), as does declaring how she expects him to treat herself and other women (male = respectful). With a daughter, what the single parent mother models with other men and expects her daughter to follow has a formative effect (female = independent). What she teaches that daughter about acceptable and unacceptable treatment from men also counts for a lot (female = not being used or abused).

In addition, single-parent mothers can support a child's contact with significant male members of the extended family, and with other trusted male figures from their social world, from school, from outside activities, from church, or from wherever a positive influence can be drawn. Each male presence provides an adult model that the child can helpfully use as a reference for his or her own development.

One common fear some single-parent mothers have is that their son, lacking a father and identifying with the mother, may somehow form a sexual preference for male partners. *There is simply no scientifically established evidence that links a son's homosexuality to his single-parent mothering.*

If the single parent is a father, and the mother is missing, then the daughter is at risk of self-defining based on female stereotypes, whereas the son may look to opposite sex peers to provide the primary female attachment he is missing.

23

^^

TELEVISION

THE BEST COMMUNICATOR IN THE FAMILY

Because television commands more attention than anyone else in the household, the single parent may as well consider it as another member of the family and treat it accordingly. Make sure what it says is within the bounds of what is considered appropriate for children to see and hear, and don't let it interfere with everyone else's communication. Sometimes television can monopolize conversation and get in the way of other family members listening or speaking up.

All of this is easier said than done because there is no one in the family who can communicate as entertainingly as the television. Try eating supper together with the television on, and conversation with each other becomes turned off. Try to get an answer to a question, and the other person doesn't seem to hear. Try to speak up about something important, and the best available attention is the side of the other person's head. Try to interrupt and get some help or remind the children about a chore, and they plead for a delay. "Wait 'til this program's over!" Then, after the single parent has waited as requested, by the time he or she asks again, another program has begun. "Not now!" the children object.

Like all technology, television is a mixed blessing. On the positive side, it is a pipeline to popular culture, a window on events occurring in an ever-changing world, an education in every imaginable facet of human experience, a source of infinite information, a marketplace to sell and shop for new products, a teller of endless stories, a constantly available escape from drudgery and the trials of daily life, a family of familiar characters that can provide a sense of social company, a baby-sitter to distract and subdue restless children, a stimulant to wake up with, and a soporific to put one to sleep. It's hard to imagine life without it.

On the down side, however, there are some costs that the single parent must consider and some questions he or she must ask.

- As an *activity*, does watching television interfere with meaningful communication, needed cooperation, or engaging in other constructive pursuits?
- As an *influence*, does some content on television expose children to programming that violates the single parent's family values?
- Does it condition them to treat unacceptable behavior as okay?
- Does it encourage them to embrace negative beliefs and imitate the negative conduct they see?

If the answer to any of these questions is "yes," then the single parent needs to limit viewing, monitor what is being watched, and take the time to editorialize with children about the implications of what they see.

Frequently, marital tensions leading up to divorce can cause families to depend on television to escape from conflict by reducing interpersonal communication. Whoever got home first turned on the television, and whoever went to bed last turned it off. When parents didn't want to argue, one or both would watch television. When they did choose to argue, children were told to go and watch television. When they had to assemble as a family, television kept them apart while they were together. They could focus on the program, not on each other. When the painful reality of family life became hard to take, the desire to seek refuge from that reality increased. The more unhappy everyone felt, the more isolated they became, relying on television to create the barrier for separation that was needed.

Once divorce is final, the single parent may need to restructure the role of television to put it back in its proper place—as a servant, not as a master—as something that enhances and does not interfere with the quality of family life. Against the protests of children who have gotten out of the habits of conversing, helping, cooperating, and entertaining themselves, the parent locks the television away for a week. "Until we can function well without it, we're not going to watch television. And when we do start watching it again, we shall only continue to do so as long as our family is working the way it should." Unplug the tube and children can feel disconnected. Like people suffering the loss of a dependency, they may feel anxious, bored, or irritated for awhile, which can be a lesson in itself.

It is hard to keep television in a healthy family place, but it can be done. The single parent has to lead the way. Most important, do not sacrifice the quality of family communication simply because this technological marvel entertains so well. Thus, when something important needs to be discussed, the single parent needs to take a stand for clear channel communication: talking with the television off.

24

~~~~~~

THE PUSH FOR INDEPENDENCE

WHY THE HARD HALF OF PARENTING COMES LAST

Adolescence refers to the eight-to-ten-year period of growth that begins with the separation from childhood (roughly between the ages of nine and thirteen) and ends with the entry into young adulthood (roughly between the ages of twenty-two and twenty-four). This is the hard half of parenting because as the adolescent pulls away, pushes against, and gets around parental authority in search of social independence and worldly experience, parents encounter more uncertainty and opposition than they faced before. They feel less in control and more embattled as a built-in conflict of interests now defines the relationship between them and their teenager.

On the adolescent side, healthy growth impels teenagers to press for all the freedom they can get as soon as they get it. On the parental side, fathers and mothers must undertake the thankless role of restraining that push for independence within the interests of safety and responsibility. Although the natural opposition makes for an abrasive time in the parent/child relationship, the intermittent conflict itself is serving a purpose. By wearing down mutual tolerance for dependence between them, this abrasion eventually leads teenagers to give up relying on their parents for support, and parents to relinquish taking care of their child.

Adolescence is bounded by two separations. The first is from childhood into adolescence itself. The second is from adolescence into adulthood, young people at last resolved to manage on their own. For even the most devoted mothers and fathers, adolescence can wear the magic out of parenting. Enchanted by their child during the first half of their parenting, they become gradually disenchanted by their teenager during the second half, until they are ready to let go of their son or daughter and he or she is ready to let go of them. Independence is like an amicable divorce that allows both parties to separate in order to improve their relationship.

Even with two parents present, a hard-charging, highly intense teenager can be a handful. Single parents fighting the battle for a responsible independence alone can find it lonely and exhausting work. This is why, during the hard half of parenting, they must find other adult support with whom to share the perplexity and duress, and from whom to get encouragement and helpful ideas. Their children's adolescence is no time for single parents to go it alone. This is not to say that single parents are obligated to go through an agony of aggravation with each teenager. They are not. About one third of children seem to journey through adolescence without much need for opposition or correction. Another third usually require occasional reining in. A final third, however, seem to press all the buttons and test all the limits. If parents going through this *third-degree adolescence* feel as if the harder they try the harder things get, they should seek outside help that can restore communication and cooperation in the family.

What changes, then, will inform single parents that their child has entered adolescence? There are four kinds of changes.

1. *Characteristics* change: Physically and socially the child appears and acts more adult.

2. *Values* change: Beliefs and tastes counter to parental culture are adopted.
3. *Habits* change: Inconsiderate patterns of behavior are adopted that parents find harder to tolerate.
4. *Wants* change: Freedoms become more urgently demanded and more difficult to grant.

In addition, living with the adolescent feels different than living with the child. Whereas the child may have been loving, obedient, hard working, and helpful, the adolescent tends to be more resistant, uncooperative, unmotivated, and moody. Single parents also observe some changes in themselves. With the child, they used to be understanding, patient, trustful, and fun loving, but with the adolescent they have become worrying, critical, questioning, and tense—all of which is normal. Change in the child begets change in the parent. As a consequence, their relationship is altered.

The challenge of single parenting the adolescent is keeping the relationship lovingly together while the parent and the child are growing apart. This separation is necessary. It provides the teenager room to grow so independence can be learned. As for the hard times that inevitably arise, single parents need to remember that *adolescence is not a punishable offense.* It is a process of growth. They must accept the process while holding the teenager accountable for the choices he or she makes. Remember, *teenagers are naturally offensive* because the process of adolescence is by definition an oppositional one. Always at issue is the matter of freedom: single parents gradually letting the teenager go if they are given adequate time to think, reliable data to trust, and evidence of responsibility to count on.

25

‸‸

EARLY ADOLESCENCE

THE CHANGE FOR THE WORSE

Sometime between the ages of nine and thirteen, the entry into adolescence usually begins. What parents typically notice is a change in their son or daughter's energy, attitude, and behavior.

This was the child who used to be extremely active, interested in many things, always on the go. Suddenly, it is as if someone pulled a plug and all this positive energy has been drained away. The child has entered *developmental lumphood*. Lying around, complaining about being bored, and being at loose ends with nothing to do, the child is unhappy being passive but unwilling to be active. He or she does not appreciate helpful suggestions from parents, shooting all these ideas down to prove that parents are no longer of any use. "No, I don't want to do that! You don't understand! Just leave me alone!"

Then, as positive energy is lost, negative energy begins to build. The child seems to become discontent with everything, critical of everyone, communicating complaints that begin irritating other family members who sometimes criticize in return, only increasing the child's negativity. Parents who could previously do no wrong in their child's eyes, now can do no right. What's going on?

Negativity

The opening shot of adolescence is *the birth of the bad attitude*, this pervasive negativity that parents now observe.

People don't initiate change in themselves unless they are dissatisfied with who and how they are, and this is true for the early adolescent. The boy or girl is dissatisfied with being defined and being treated any longer as a child. He or she wants to relinquish this old identity and find a new one—older, more grown up, more adult. This self-dissatisfaction provides the motivation to change, propelling the adolescent out of childhood by rejecting the old definition of child.

This is a *negative* decision. The adolescent knows how he or she *doesn't* want to be, but has no clear idea of a positive image to happily inhabit. What is clear is the determination to be different. "I'm different from how I was." "I no longer want to be treated as a child." "I'm different from how you are as my parents." "I'm going to be different from how you want me to be." Directly spoken or implied by conduct, all these declarations of becoming different are statements of *separation*. The adolescent is resolved to leave childhood behind. Opposed to the old definition, opposed to the old way of being treated, the adolescent becomes more oppositional to live with.

For the first time, the adolescent realizes the full impact of parental and social rules. They are imposed by others to limit his or her personal freedom at a time when more freedom is what is wanted. Now the negative attitude becomes intensified into a *grievance* against all those who stand in the way of the adolescent's freedom to grow. This is unfair! Why should adult authorities be allowed to restrict his or her independence with demands? Angrily the adolescent confronts the parent: "You have no to right to tell me what to do! You're not the boss of the world!" *Early adolescent outrage* is a response to recognizing limits that the child quietly observed before, but will accept no longer without complaint.

Rebellion

Once the adolescent has reached this state of grievance, he or she is ready for the next phase of early adolescence, *rebellion*. People don't rebel without a sense of just cause and now, with a chip on the shoulder, the adolescent feels justified in defending personal freedom and contesting adult authority. Through rebellion he or she gathers the power to change, actively resisting requests by argument, passively resisting them by endless delay. "I said I'll do it and I will. In a minute!" Early adolescent "minutes" can last for hours. *Resistance works.* Through the use of stubborn opposition and relentless procrastination, the adolescent is able to create more freedom. Through arguing against "right now" or promising to do it "later," he or she can sometimes escape parental demands when a father or mother is too weary to maintain a stand or follow through and check on what has been requested.

Experimentation

Armed with this new sense of power, the adolescent enters the final phase of early adolescence, *experimentation*. Experiment with what? With a host of new experiences that were beyond the boundaries of childhood, are now within the reach of adolescence, and are likely to be disapproved of by parents. Sometimes it seems that early adolescents, by asserting differentness, are courting adult disapproval, and in a way they are. "If my parents don't like my new hairstyle, I know it must look cool." There is no recognition of early adolescence more eagerly sought than parental disapproval because it certifies that the boy or girl is truly becoming different from the child he or she was. For this reason, parents should feel free to express disagreement with any new belief or behavior to which they authentically take offense, being careful not to demean or reject the child in the process. Parental disapproval proves adolescent differentiation is taking place.

Parents should be prepared for many kinds of changes in their child. There will be different styles of dressing, alternative tastes in popular music, underground interests and ideals, countercultural beliefs and attitudes, and daring and different friends. Parents should not be afraid to draw the line when differences exceed their tolerance or threaten the safety of the child. Even if the early adolescent backs off and gives in to a parental prohibition and appears to lose, he or she has actually won. The statement of difference has been made and he or she has caught the parent's attention.

Added to this experimentation with social image and relationships is curiosity about those adult freedoms that signify, like a rite of passage, that one is no longer a child. A whole world of unchildlike possibilities has opened up. These include many activities that carry significant risk. Early adolescents may try breaking the law by shoplifting, pranking, or vandalizing. They may try substance use by smoking cigarettes, sniffing inhalants, drinking alcohol. They may begin sexual activity by making out and fondling. Frightening to parents, these risk-taking activities are fascinating to their teenager, who proceeds with impunity because he or she is protected against these risks by *denial*. "Oh don't worry. I know all about that. Accidents aren't going to happen to me!" What parents want to prohibit, the early adolescent wants to experience.

What are parents to do? Parents should state their values, openly discuss the risks, increase their surveillance, and when harm occurs, allow enough of the consequences to be felt and faced so bad experience becomes a good teacher.

The negative attitude, the rebellion, and the beginning of experimentation are all hallmarks of early adolescence—signs that most single parents do not welcome. If this period in the adolescent's life coincides with parental divorce, these signs may become more strongly expressed and more difficult for single parents to manage. In hurt and anger, an early adolescent child of divorce may become more than normally negative, rebellious, and experimental, acting out painful feelings as a way of striking back. If this reaction occurs, it requires a combination of extreme sensitivity and strong stands from single parents to help the adolescent from doing himself or herself injury. He or she can become so negative that important relationships are alienated, so rebellious that significant self-interests are given up, and so recklessly experimental that well-being is placed in danger.

The challenge of single parenting an early adolescent is to insist on acceptable behaviors during an oppositional time, to maintain positive contact between corrective encounters, not to take negativity personally, and not to punish the adolescent for the process of separation that has begun. As the early adolescent discovers a more positive self-definition, he or she will begin to become a more positive presence in the family.

26

~~~~~~

MID-ADOLESCENCE

THE SHELL OF SELF-CENTEREDNESS

Between the ages of thirteen and sixteen, signs of mid-adolescence usually appear. Increasingly self-preoccupied, the teenager becomes less considerate of family. As social freedom to grow assumes maximum importance, he or she can become quickly combative when denied. Delay of any gratification is painful because the sense of urgency is so intense. Frustration is easily aroused. The teenager feels he or she must have what is wanted, as soon as it is wanted, which means *now*.

Exploiting Freedom

A certain ruthlessness becomes apparent. Worldly freedoms are too important to be denied. When parents won't allow permission for what the teenager wants, he or she is prepared to sneak around their authority. This is the age of the *end run*. The teenager will promise he or she is going where parents have agreed, only to go elsewhere, which has been forbidden. Two teenagers may tell their respective parents each is going to spend the night at the other's house, and then both use the freedom lying brings to enjoy a night's adventure on the town. It is the age of *playing loopholes* with one's parent. What freedoms parents don't explicitly prohibit, the teenager takes as tacit permission, exploiting technicalities in the law. "Well, you never said I couldn't!" the teenager innocently exclaims. "Because I never thought you would!" replies the parent who now establishes a prohibition where there was none before: "Well, I'm telling you now. Using my charge card is not allowed." Of course, the teenager actually knew this without having to be told, but temptation of the moment ruled.

It is the age of *social extortion*. Waiting until the last minute to request permission, and backed up by the presence of impatient friends who are eager to leave, the teenager asks: "Can I go to the concert?" Will pressure in a public situation, with no time to weigh the risks, cause the parent to impulsively give in? The teenager hopes so. Instead, the parent demands time to think and privacy to talk. "If you want me to consider letting you go, tell your friends to wait while you and I discuss my concerns in the next room."

It is the age where the punishment is often worth the crime. Pay for fun now by facing consequences later. It is the age when the teenager will promise anything to gain freedom now, only to renege on that promise later, after the freedom has been enjoyed. It is the age where parents play detective, asking questions invasive of the teenager's privacy to satisfy their need to know. All the while the teenager gives evasive answers to protect that privacy, believing that the less parents know, the less likely they are to interfere. It is the age when the teenager cannot tolerate delay of personal gratification, yet possesses an infinite capacity for delay (procrastination) when it comes to satisfying demands from parents.

Delaying Permission

To be single parenting during this period in a child's life is enormously demanding. The lack of consideration can feel so irritating and the risks that the teenager wants to take can feel so frightening. For example, is the child sufficiently attentive and responsible to be allowed behind the wheel of a car? This question needs to be asked and answered, because at age sixteen many teenagers are still mid-adolescent. If parents answer: "No, my child is too impulsive and inattentive to be ready," then delay permission to use a car. Just because a teenager has reached the legal age to be licensed does not mean parents are legally bound to let the adolescent drive.

Letting teenagers drive is like adding a rocket to their thrust for independence. The same can be said for allowing them to date or to hold a part-time job. "If I have a car, then I can go anywhere I want." "If I date, then I am entitled to act grown-up in other ways." "If I make my own money, then I should be able to make my own decisions." All three activities dramatically intensify the teenager's push for freedom. Single parents must be willing to delay permission until they feel their teenager can handle these responsibilities. If a single parent has a mid-adolescent who is not responsibly taking care of business at home, at school, or out in the world, *do not let the teenager drive, date, or have a part-time job.*

To single parents of a teenager at this frustrated and frustrating age, it seems as if their child has become encapsulated in a shell of self-centeredness. Having entered the most intense period of adolescent growth, the teenager can think about little else than satisfying the social craving for more freedom and new experience. Now the period of thankless parenting begins, as parents must take stands for the teenager's best interests against what he or she passionately wants, stands that their sons and daughters resent and resist. What is it about being told "no" that the teenager cannot accept? When it comes to freedom, no reasons are good enough to justify refusal. For their loyal opposition, single parents receive anger and conflict as reward.

Now the teenager pushes and parents restrain that push as tension and conflict become part of daily life. For a time, the relationship can feel truly disaffected. Parents and teenager love each other still, but often do not like each other very much. To preserve precious freedom from restrictive consequences of wrongdoing, the teenager may lie, blame, make excuses, or deny what actually occurred. In opposition, single parents must confront these cover-ups, demanding truth, applying consequences, and expecting the teenager to recover the situation in order to learn responsibility for mistakes or misdeeds.

Speaking Up and Holding Firm

All children grow up partly within and partly outside the bounds of acceptable behavior that their parents set. No child tells the truth or all of the truth to parents all the time. If parenting is going to get hard, mid-adolescence is often when this hardship occurs, with the mother or father regularly having to deal with out-of-bounds behavior, lying, and conflict during this period of their child's growth. Single parents must firmly assert authority and insist on honesty to protect the teenager from acting without adequate caution or self-restraint.

Parental popularity with the teenager at this critical period is not the issue. The teenager's safety is what matters. Whenever parents are in doubt about what the teenager is saying or wanting to do, *delay and think, question and find out, check and verify, search and discover, push for what's right, and feel free to say "no."* The likelihood is that later, when the teenager is out of adolescence and looking back, he or she will appreciate the loyal single parent who courageously spoke up and held firm when all the teenager could think about was pushing him or her away, and breaking free.

27

~~~~~~

LATE ADOLESCENCE

THE UNREADINESS FOR INDEPENDENCE

With the onset of late adolescence—roughly between the ages of sixteen and nineteen—the teenager enters an anxious time. The twin luxuries of not having to think beyond present gratification and depending totally on his or her parent for support are coming to an end. In a couple of years or less, whether in school or not, the age of high school graduation brings with it expectations for more independence, more serious thought about the future, and the reality of soon leaving home.

In response to these concerns, troublesome questions now begin to plague the teenager's mind:

- "Will I be ready for independence?"
- "What is my next step?"
- "What do I want to do with my life?"
- "How will I manage on my own?"
- "Will I see my friends again?"
- "What happens if I mess up?"

These are questions without answers and they fill the teenager with doubt. When parents ask about their son or daughter's plans, the teenager may either avoid the subject or become irritable. When the teenager seems to regress in social behavior, acting younger and putting off important preparations like filling out job or college applications, parents worry that their child is reluctant to finally grow up, which is the truth. Instead, the teenager would rather deny the frightening reality of impending independence and act as if it will go away. Except he or she knows it won't.

What helps reduce fear of unreadiness in late adolescence is for parents to gradually transfer most self-regulation and more financial self-support to the teenager as graduation time nears. During the last year or so of living at home, their son or daughter should approximate full freedom of independence while still being expected to meet some family membership requirements for helping out and keeping parents adequately informed. This means that as the end of his or her stay at home approaches, parents systematically turn over obligations like schoolwork, let go of some protective restraints like setting curfew, and expect more reliance for self-support from earning expenses through summer and part-time employment. Should the teenager stumble in meeting any of these demands, parents don't rush in and take charge. Instead, they let their son or daughter confront and recover from the consequences. They treat the teenager as grown-up enough to accept adult responsibility for his or her choices, a capacity they want to maximize before the late adolescent child leaves their care.

Ambivalence
The teenager wants this respect on the one hand, and doesn't want it on the other. The ambivalence expressed to parents is confusing, but honest: "Let me alone to run my life, but be there for me when I need helping out." The teenager feels truly mixed about this transition into independence. Looking forward to no longer being subject to parental supervision and being free to live by personal choice, he or she still regrets giving up parental support and having to rely on personal resources. The price of freedom and independence is a certain amount of loneliness and fear. Complaints about

being overprotected now give way to anxieties from feeling unprotected. "Suppose my car breaks down and I don't have the money to fix it? How am I going to get to my job?"

As the time for separation approaches, parents can help plan the next step by offering advice when, based on their experience, they foresee pitfalls that the teenager does not. Now begins that transformation of parents from people who didn't know anything at all, into people who surprisingly seem to know a whole lot.

At this time, parents also need to clarify the degree, duration, and conditions of their continuing support so the teenager knows on what he or she can rely. Most important, single parents must restrain themselves from voicing any worry they may feel, confiding it to friends but *not* the teenager.

Unwavering Faith

In late adolescence parental worry is received as a vote of no confidence. This, the teenager doesn't need. He or she has enough self-doubt already. What the teenager needs from a single parent at this point is just the opposite: unwavering faith that the son or daughter has what it takes to negotiate the next step into independence, to make good choices, and to recover from those that turn out badly.

That the teenager is not completely ready for this step is not a problem. It is to be expected. Probably the most preparation any parents can give is not more than 60 percent of the skills, understanding, and practice needed to cope in the world. If parents refuse to release their teenager until the child is fully ready, they will never let their son or daughter go. The late adolescent must leave *before* he or she is completely ready. To learn the rest, the almost-grown child is turned over to The Big R, *Reality*, that finishes instruction the hard way, through sometimes painful experience. This is really no different than how learning about life is conducted during adulthood. No one can be fully prepared for all the challenges life brings. The trick is staying ready to be challenged. Just like single parents, the late adolescent has to cope with the unexpected as he or she grows along life's way.

28

‸‸‸

TRIAL INDEPENDENCE

THE CHALLENGE OF LIVING ON ONE'S OWN

If single parents are fortunate, their son or daughter will grow through the last phase of adolescence, trial independence (roughly between ages eighteen and twenty-three), away from home. Renting a room, sharing an apartment, living in a dormitory, the young person confronts the reality of living on one's own for the first time and usually finds it more challenging than expected, particularly having so much freedom for temptation.

This is the age of slipping and sliding, as most young people make and break one or more of a whole string of commitments—leases, credit agreements, bank accounts, legal obligations, caring relationships, academic programs, job requirements, promises to oneself and to others. Trying to keep everything together usually proves too much. There is so much one should do that one would rather not, and there is so much one wants to do that one is eager to try. Sooner or later, lack of responsibility, overdoing pleasure, or both, causes the young man or woman's world to crisis. What is he or she going to do now?

Meanwhile, all around are friends at the same stage of life struggling to find their footing too, everyone discovering that a working independence requires a lot of discipline and self-restraint. Not only is there the requirement of self-support, there is also learning to live on society's terms. Here they thought they would be free at last, only to discover the opposite. Now they are accountable for becoming informed about and following a host of social rules and social requirements, like laws and taxes, that they could afford to ignore when still living at home. Trial independence is the time for learning just how much work is involved in totally taking care of themselves.

It doesn't help matters that these three to five years after high school are often when peak alcohol and drug use occur, as well as sexual acting out, encouraging good times now that must be paid for later. All in all, it is a mercy for parents to be kept in ignorance about the adventures and misadventures in the life of their child during this wild time before finally settling down into young adulthood.

Whereas some young people catch hold of responsibility as soon as they enter trial independence, many do not. Stumbling and falling, they reach out to their parent for support to help them cope with difficulty or to take them back in. At these times, if aid is to be given, parents need to make it conditional on the young person doing a major share of the recovery. The parent is there to help, but not to rescue. If the young person comes home, it needs to be understood that the duration of this stay is limited. The parent is providing the son or daughter an opportunity to regroup: to rethink, to recover, and to get ready to reenter the world on independent terms. This is not a time to retreat, to give up, or to lapse back into an indefinite dependence on parental care.

There is no sin in needing help during trial independence, nor in not successfully establishing independence the first time out. Parents need to reflect this understanding in their attitude. They should not despair; they should show faith. They should not punish; they should be patient. They should not criticize; they should consult. Their job is to help the young person accept and understand the difficulties of independent living, to respect their son or daughter for struggling with that challenge, and to encourage getting back out and struggling some more.

The challenges are real. Just having a roommate for the first time is a lesson in interdependent living. Sharing the joint use of space, cooperating with each other's needs, depending on mutual commitments, tolerating differences, communicating in disagreement, living with someone you don't always like, and resolving conflict are all part of the informal education that this period of trial independence brings.

In time, the slipping and sliding diminishes, firmer footing is found, and more control over one's life is gained. At this point, entry into young adulthood has begun, childhood and adolescence are over, and the parent's active parenting is done.

29

‹‹

ACHIEVEMENT IS IMPORTANT, BUT

KEEPING PERFORMANCE IN PERSPECTIVE

No question, school achievement is important. It supports present self-esteem and enables future mobility. Achievement however, is only one part of a child's development. There are many other important areas of growth: social, emotional, moral, spiritual, physical, artistic, expressive, and relational, to name a few. There is much more to children than school performance. After all, they are human beings, not just human doers. This can be difficult to remember, however, in a culture that often defines worth based on performance, extols excellence, and rewards winning with success. Sometimes it is useful to recall President Harry Truman's observation: "'C' students rule the world." It takes more than good grades to rise to prominence.

To allow academics to measure how the child is performing overall can lead parents to conclusions that are not necessarily so. All "A's" do not guarantee that their son or daughter is responsible, hard working, healthily adjusted, happy, generally well behaved, is good at everything else, is even interested in learning, or is going to be successful in later life. Some of these assumptions may be true, but some may not. It is best for parents not to make these automatic linkages. Instead, evaluate each area of growth independently.

Another linkage to beware is the dangerous equation, parent = child. This equivalence can imply that the conduct of a child depends on parenting received, and that parenting is evaluated by the performance of the child. Thus, if the child does well, the parent should be credited for doing a good job, whereas if the child does badly, that parent should be criticized for falling down on the job. To use the child to measure the parent's performance creates two unhappy outcomes. Either the child is burdened with responsibility for making the parent look good, or the child is blamed for making the parent look bad.

Single parents, because they have no partner with whom to share daily responsibility for the children, are often very concerned about their own performance. Are they doing enough? Are they doing right? To avoid enmeshment in their son or daughter's school achievement, they need to make a strong, unequivocal declaration of independence to the child about the issue of his or her performance. The statement can sound something like this: "Independently of how you choose to perform at school, I feel good about myself as your parent and you as my child. When you perform well, I do not take the credit. When you perform badly, I do not take the blame. My responsibility is to guide and support you the best I can, but your choices are your responsibility to make."

A final linkage to beware is represented by a common parental statement of congratulations: "I'm proud of you!" Although this response may be received as a general declaration of approval, it may also invoke the parent = child linkage in a damaging way. It can misappropriate the primary benefit of the child's achievement to the parent by suggesting "because of how you did, I feel good about myself as a parent." Now the child may be encouraged to believe that personal performance supports not only his or her own

KEYS TO SINGLE PARENTING

esteem, but the parent's as well. Conversely, should personal performance drop, the child may feel threatened by the loss of parental pride, *disappointment*.

That statement, "I am disappointed in you" (or "with you" or "for you"), can have a devastating effect. Not only must the child recover from some degree of failure, to regain parental approval he or she must also work to make up for letting parents down so they can recover lost esteem. Better for parents to give congratulations for a job well done by expressing approval in a nonentangling way. They can simply say "good for you," or "you did well." If parents feel the child performed below capacity and want to say so, they can omit any reference to personal disappointment. "This was not as good as I believe you are capable of doing."

As for communicating expectations about achievement, particularly concerning grades, they should be concrete, not abstract. General statements like "just do your best," "try your hardest," "perform up to your potential," leave the child to interpret exactly what standard is sufficient. But how can children know for sure if they are doing their best, trying their hardest, or living up to their potential? They can't. Nobody can. They can, however, place a lot of pressure on themselves by striving for standards that remain undefined.

It is best for single parents to *specify* what level of performance is realistic for the child and satisfactory to them. "I don't know the maximum grades you are capable of achieving, but these are the minimum grades I will accept. Should you fall below the minimum, I will step in to help you rise above it."

30

~~~~~~

ENCOURAGING EDUCATION

KEEPING THE FAMILY SAFE FOR LEARNING

Most single parents support their child's education because they believe that learning increases competence and enhances self-esteem. This conviction is true except when the experience of education is conducted in a manner that inhibits the desire to learn. A lot depends upon the teacher, and the most powerful teachers of all are parents. Parental instruction in the home shapes much of the child's attitude toward learning, and toward other teachers he or she may encounter.

The willingness to learn is easily discouraged because *learning can feel risky.* If the risks lead to injury, the child may refuse to learn. What risks? To acquire a skill or understanding one does not possess, one must admit *ignorance,* make *mistakes,* feel *stupid,* look *foolish,* and then get *evaluated* for one's efforts. No wonder young children will frequently resist attempting what they have never attempted before or are not already good at. The risks get in the way. Children become scared of trying. Although learning builds self-esteem, it also takes self-esteem to risk learning.

Parents as teachers are often insensitive to the child's plight because they suffer from *instructional amnesia.* This is a common human problem that afflicts many adults. As soon as people have practiced a skill or mastered an understanding, they tend to forget how difficult it was to learn. When sitting down with an elementary school child slow to comprehend his or her homework, parents may have a hard time understanding their son's or daughter's difficulty because the assignment seems very simple to them. Whatever is the matter with the child? Nothing. The parents have just forgotten what their own initial learning experience was like. They have grown out of touch with fears of learning that their child is experiencing now.

The challenge of encouraging education requires that parents be mindful of difficulty they do not remember, and act to make learning *safe* by reducing its inherent risks. There are several ways in which parents can help create this security:

1. They can give ignorance permission by declaring: "It's okay not to know. All learning starts with ignorance."
2. They can treat mistakes as efforts: "Good for you for trying. Try again."
3. They can be sensitive to feelings of stupidity: "It's scary doing what you've never done before."
4. They can admire the willingness to look foolish: "You're brave to let others watch as you struggle to learn."
5. Independent of outcome, they can always give a positive evaluation: "Now you know more than you did before."

What can discourage learning is when parents become impatient, thus increasing the risks. They can do this by putting down ignorance: "You should know this already." They can become frustrated by mistakes: "Why can't you do it right the first time?" They can criticize stupidity: "How can you be so dumb?" They can embarrass effort and arouse feelings of foolishness: "Even a three-year-old could learn this faster than you." They can give a punitive evaluation: "Well, this just goes to show you'll never learn to do it right." If out of fatigue or from other stress, single parents ever find themselves in danger of making these kinds of responses to their child, they should disengage from the child's project and declare time for a break. *Do not try to help educate the child when you feel emotionally unprepared to encourage.*

Modeling also matters. When parents criticize and get angry at themselves for making mistakes, when they call themselves names or otherwise become upset because they can't figure out what they need to know or want to fix, they are demonstrating that difficulty in learning lowers self-esteem. In addition, they are showing the child that if one can't learn quickly and easily, then something must be the matter with the learner.

Siblings also need attention if the family is to be kept safe for learning. Many times, to assert dominance or from a desire to tease, older children will demean the efforts of younger brothers and sisters who are struggling to learn something new. Single parents need to disallow this interference. The message to every child in the family must be extremely clear: *Learning is too important to let anyone discourage others from taking the necessary risks.*

31

^^

THE EARLY GRADES

SOCIALIZING AND SOCIAL CRUELTY

E ducation is the announced purpose of school. To young children, however, making and managing a social place in which to comfortably fit, holding that place, and trading up or being traded down seem to comprise the classroom experience as they journey through elementary school. Although the demands of homework also grow in the upper grades, so does the complexity of peer relationships. Usually around grades three through six, the child passes through a period of *social cruelty* when personal insecurity and the ruthless quest for popularity can cause students to be mean to each other in ways that they were not before.

Teasing becomes the order of the day. It feels better to torment others for certain qualities and characteristics before such vulnerable traits get assigned to you. Teasing is not an aggressive act; it is a defensive one. Making fun of other people becomes a serious game to play, cracking put-downs that are funny to everyone except the target of the humor, who feels hurt. Words are the weapons of choice, attacking to pre-empt attack, spreading rumors behind other people's backs, sending slanderous notes, and gossiping over the phone at night. Whatever social innocence a child had in the early elementary grades is lost when cliques begin to form. Then *social meanness* becomes the order of the day, a tactic to keep aspiring others out, whereas *social niceness* is used by people wanting to get in. Leaders of this social cruelty act like bullies, followers act like cowards (fearfully joining in lest they get teased), and targets of this treatment feel like victims.

Single parents need to watch their child's social adjustment in the later elementary grades to make sure he or she is not getting seriously hurt or seriously hurting others. Both experiences can have a formative effect. If the child is a constant victim of injurious teasing, self-esteem can suffer, causing withdrawal for protection. Expression of vulnerable feelings may become discouraged, thereby creating an unwillingness to speak up or stand out. The child may begin keeping people at a distance, becoming more private and hard to know. In the extreme, he or she can fear embarrassment and feel ashamed, isolating the child on both counts.

Should single parents see their child incurring any of these costs, there are some helpful responses they can give:

1. They can listen to the hurt feelings so the child has a chance to talk the suffering out in safety.
2. They can help the child make sure not to act in ways that provoke or reinforce the cruel treatment.
3. They can provide perspective by explaining how this treatment has to do with the age, not the child's person.
4. They can explain that as classmates grow older, the need to treat each other badly will diminish as everyone starts feeling more secure.
5. They can support the social courage it takes for the child to go to school knowing the hard experience to come.
6. They can encourage, even help practice, taking a more socially aggressive stand against this treatment if persistently ignoring cruelty has failed to make it go away.

7. They can help the child to not take this mistreatment personally by believing it is deserved because he or she is a bad or inferior person.
8. They can encourage the child to engage in outside-of-school activities and to join other social circles that offer relationships supportive of self-esteem.

Finally, as a last resort, they can intervene with the classroom teacher by asking that the incidence of social cruelty at school be addressed. The teacher can let all the students know that this treatment of each other is not acceptable and will not be tolerated. This prohibition is consistent with the teacher's role, because he or she already has in place some rules for communication and conduct in the classroom.

As for the child who comes to enjoy being socially cruel to classmates, parents also need to address this behavior. To learn to feel good by making others feel bad, and to learn to be socially dominant at all costs are not approaches that will serve the child well in caring relationships later in life. More to the point, learning to gang up on, to intimidate, to bully, to torment, to humiliate, to exclude, to name call, to slander, or to vandalize are all behaviors that can carry over to harmful effect in the family. This message to this child must be clear. "Just because your classmates treat each other badly at school does not mean you can treat your brother and sister that way at home."

32

THE LATER GRADES

THE DEMANDS FOR FITTING IN
AND SELF-RESPONSIBILITY

When children begin middle school or junior high, they enter an institutional world that will treat them very differently from the elementary school they left behind. They will find themselves to be a smaller part of a larger, more impersonal organization. There, they will have more teachers who, because of having more students, will know them less well. In consequence, teachers may have less patience, be less nurturing, expect more obedience, demand more work, enforce more rules, and seem to some children more "mean."

Parents of a student this age will have their own adjustments to make. If they were highly involved in their child's elementary school, and if that relationship felt intimate and supportive in response, they may go through some withdrawal come junior high. "This isn't Kansas anymore." They have to let go of their cozy connection with that smaller school. They must readjust their expectations to fit a larger, harder place. Now they will tend to get less information, have less easy access to the principal and teachers, have less influence over what happens to their child, and need more persistence and tact should they want to advocate for the child within the system.

This does not mean that secondary school teachers do not care about students or are not responsive to parents. It only recognizes the reality that these teachers have instructional responsibility for more children, most of whom have now entered early adolescence. These two factors affect how mid-level teachers tend to treat students, and how students tend to treat them. An adolescent is no longer a child. A secondary school is no longer an elementary school.

In general, elementary school children were far easier to teach. Many were curious, industrious, attentive, enthusiastic, positive, cooperative, and friendly. By middle school, however, students can be much more challenging to instruct. As a function of early adolescence, many are disinterested, indolent, distracted, apathetic, negative, rebellious, or even hostile. The result is that secondary teachers are often more frustrated by students and less responsive to parents than their elementary counterparts. In a school whose mission is to partly help students learn sufficient self-discipline to prepare for high school, there is a population of young people at an age where schoolwork feels more distasteful, regulation feels more oppressive, and authority feels more unfair.

Sometimes it seems like school systems should just declare a moratorium on education during early adolescence. Instead, give children a few more years to grow up and then reintroduce instruction when they have become more tractable again. However, middle school has more than just academics to teach. Students have much to learn about working within a system to advance their interests. *Cooperating* with teachers, *complying* with rules, and *conforming* to institutional norms—all in the interests of getting students' educational needs met—are critical skills to master at this negative and oppositional age.

Students who fail to learn these social skills in middle school are at higher risk of not making it through high school. An even larger institution than middle school, high school is more demanding of work and responsibility, and less patient with resistance and infraction. In many public educational systems, the freshman year of high school is the grade in which the highest drop-out rate occurs. Not only are students academically unprepared from lack of previous application, more important, they are socially unprepared to accept the stricter demands for cooperation, conformity, and compliance that await them.

When an angry early adolescent gets in trouble at junior high, being sent from class to the office, into in-school suspension, assigned after-school detention, or given suspension from school itself, parents do *not* need to double-punish the offense at home. School consequences are usually sufficient. Parents do have a role, however, in verifying what happened with the school and, assuming that they feel the infraction was real and the punishment was justified, in helping the child understand the connection between the misbehavior committed and the consequence that followed. Parents need to support the school's policies wherever they feel they honestly can. They need to do this for the child's sake, because he or she has to learn to work within an institutional system.

Why? Because as children grow older, they will have to interact with a host of institutions that make up the larger social system in which as adults they must function to get their needs met. To satisfy needs for social governance, for military service, for health, for safety, for legal redress, for financial help, for employment, and for all kinds of services, he or she must learn how to go along to get along. Unfortunately, "going along" is the last lesson many rebellious early adolescents want to learn. "What right do others have to tell me what to do? I'm not going to spend my life following orders!"

"Going along" doesn't mean becoming a robot, giving up all individuality, or forsaking any claim to independence. It doesn't mean not disagreeing, not questioning, not speaking up, or not standing up for principles and beliefs. It just means acquiring four important social learnings that junior high or middle school has to teach. Each social lesson will serve the child well in later years.

1. The child's life will always be partly governed by authorities he or she did not choose.
2. The child's conduct will always be partly regulated by rules he or she did not make.
3. There will always be others to answer to, some of whom the child may not like.
4. After a misfortune, mistake, or misdeed, there will often be social consequences that the child may consider unfair.

All lives must be lived partly on terms *not* of the individual's choosing or liking. To some degree, everyone has to learn to cooperate, conform, and comply to get their needs met in society. If the child can't begin to accept and work with this harsh fact of life in middle school, he or she is likely to have to learn it at greater cost later on.

33

‸‸‸

THE EARLY ADOLESCENT ACHIEVEMENT DROP

PREVENTING FALLING GRADES FROM FAILING EFFORT

Adolescent attitudes can dictate behaviors that interfere with school achievement. Even capable high school students can feel impelled to take a self-defeating approach toward their education. Consider just a few of the negative statements these teenagers commonly make. "It's dumb to ask questions." "It's right to beat the system." "It's smart to act stupid." "It's stupid to work hard." "It's cool not to care." "It's good to act bad." "It's enough to get by." Fortunately, as the end of high school nears, with the responsibilities for more independence fast approaching, these beliefs and behaviors begin to lose their appeal because they are detrimental to successfully moving on.

It is between the ages of nine and thirteen, however, when early adolescent attitudes begin to form, that school achievement is often placed at significant risk. The danger is created because in the process of separating from childhood, early adolescents want to define themselves differently from how they were as a child, and from how parents want them to become. Oppositionally, they rebel out of childhood to begin their journey toward social independence.

As they throw away "childish" aspects of themselves (because they no longer want to treat themselves or be treated as a child), they can alter their priorities. For example, it may be that through the early elementary grades, *achievement* was a major pillar of self-esteem as well as a valued source of parental approval. *Acceptance* from friends may have ranked next, because family was still of primary social importance. Personal *appearance* was probably a distant third. Come early adolescence, however, these personal priorities can reverse for the child. Number one becomes appearance and dress, because looks can significantly affect what is now priority number two, securing acceptance with friends. Image has a lot to do with fitting in and gaining popularity as approval from peers now becomes more socially compelling than parental opinion.

The result of these shifting priorities is that achievement now ranks a distant third. The social imperative has become overwhelmingly important. Which would early adolescents rather have, good grades or good friends? In many cases, there is no contest. Social success counts far more than academic achievement.

In consequence of this change in values, and as a result of their growing opposition to adult authority, early adolescents may dismiss schoolwork because it feels unimportant. When this rejection occurs, falling grades can result from failing effort, as attention, concentration, and motivation formerly devoted to study are invested elsewhere.

If this achievement drop happens to their child, what should parents do? Because this lessening of effort is normal, should they just accept it as predictable and let it go? *No.* Just because something is normal doesn't mean that it's okay. What about letting the child experience lowering grades, even failure, as a natural consequence of lack of effort? Maybe he or she will accept responsibility, return to study, and recover his or her commitment to achievement. Sometimes this self-correction will occur, but in most cases it will not.

The majority of early adolescents are not mature enough to learn recovery from academic failure on their own. In the worst cases, they start caring less about school-work, perform less well, miss assignments, neglect home-work, fall further behind, feel they can't catch up, become discouraged from trying, and finally give up. Now harsh consequences will take their toll. As grades drop, confidence and esteem lower, and children begin to see and treat themselves as failures.

Meanwhile, parents may have made a bad situation worse. Because rewards and punishments have failed to motivate the child, parents may run out of patience. In frustration they get angry, the child growing stubborn in response, and now a matter of performance at school turns into a power struggle at home. The harder parents push, the more intransigent the child becomes. "You can't *make* me study. I don't care how hard you punish or how angry you get!" Feeling helpless, parents don't know what else to do except lower expectations and let the child underachieve. "Just pass, that's all we ask!"

Rather than give up, parents need to try an approach that is more effective than getting emotionally upset, offering rewards, or applying punishment. Although such tactics can help boost a child's efforts, they usually fail with the early adolescent who rebelliously refuses to be browbeaten, bribed, or threatened into studying. Instead, parents must increase *supervision* over what is happening at school.

123

The most common contributors to lowering grades at this age are: lying about and not doing homework, not performing work in class, and being disruptive with other students. Parents can put a stop to all three misbehaviors. The intervention is simple and direct. At the same time the child is more oppositional to demands, he or she is extremely sensitive to the *social embarrassment* of being seen by peers at school in the company of his or her mother or father.

This is one of the more reliable tests for the onset of adolescence. The child felt happy to have a parent's company at school. The early adolescent is mortified. Being seen with one's parent at school is unwelcome because it violates the principle of social independence to which the early adolescence has now become committed.

By extending their supervision into the school, single parents are not trying to publicly humiliate their early adolescent. They are only using actions to convey what words alone have failed to communicate. The parental warning goes like this:

- "If you can't take care of business at school, I will take time off from work to help you."
- "If you can't manage to concentrate on daily instruction and avoid bothering other students, I will come and sit by you in class."
- "If you can't manage to bring your assignments home, I will meet you at school at the end of your last class. Together, we shall make the rounds of your teachers to pick the homework up."
- "If you can't manage to get the homework done by yourself, I will sit with you at the kitchen table until you get it done."
- "If you can't manage to turn the homework in, together we shall make the rounds of your teachers before classes begin, to see that they receive it."

- "If you tell me there is no homework and it turns out that there is, you and I shall have a meeting with your teacher. At this time you will have the opportunity to explain why you thought there wasn't homework when there was."
- "If you get a zero for not doing homework, you will have to make it up on the weekend before you can play, even though you will still get a zero for your efforts."

Sometimes, to help an early adolescent maintain adequate achievement, single parents have to show that they mean business by extending their supervisory presence into the child's world at school.

34

‸‸‸

REDEFINING FAMILY

PUSHING THE NONCUSTODIAL PARENT AWAY

There is a kind of *nuclear reaction* that can occur following divorce. The custodial mother or father, in an effort to establish the new family unit and adjust the children to it, pulls them close, expands his or her parenting role, and pushes the ex-spouse away to create space for this redefinition to occur.

During this period, custodial parents often want separation and privacy from the noncustodial parent to accomplish three tasks:

1. They want to reexamine and reaffirm their own parenting values, perhaps altering parenting priorities and practices from how they were before divorce.
2. They want to reassess the goals that direct the growth of themselves, their children, and the family as a whole to reflect new freedoms and necessities.
3. They want to set and defend new rules, asserting sole authority against the demands of children who may contest these limits before accepting and respecting them.

To attain these objectives, custodial parents may need to push the noncustodial parent away, no matter how well-meaning and useful his or her continued involvement in their new family may be. The sooner everyone adjusts to the reality of two parents in two separate homes, the better.

For noncustodial parents, however, this adjustment is not easy. Living apart, they must watch family grow close and change without them. They must stand by as the custodial parent expands the role of major parent. In many cases, this expansion includes taking over activities for which noncustodial parents were once responsible. Feeling replaced can feel scary. Feeling excluded can feel insecure and lonely.

Unlike the custodial mother or father, whose role as daily parent continues unbroken, noncustodial parents must give up this continuity for more occasional contact with children, agreeing to live apart from the family. Until this new role is established, they may cling to what they miss, trying to maintain their old place, not as a husband or wife but as a parent. Calling up, checking in, dropping by, offering advice, fixing things, and helping out are some of the means noncustodial parents use to maintain attachment. In response, custodial parents may find this ongoing presence intrusive. They want sufficient distance for separation to take place and independence to become established.

What to do when the noncustodial parent still clings to the family? Custodial parents need to give a double message: "I appreciate and want your continued involvement in the children's lives. However, I need you to base that involvement on their visitation with you, not by your coming by to visit here." Not only do custodial parents need adequate separation, so do the children whose reunion fantasies are fed by divorced parents who are continually seen together in the same home. "If Daddy still spends so much time over here, maybe he and Mommy will get back together after all."

The challenge of divorcing well is to emotionally end the marriage between the husband and wife while keeping the former partners together as father and mother. It is important that each is able to cooperate with the other in support of the children's growing needs. What enables this collaboration is the capacity of each partner to create a satisfying life independent of the other. Living happily apart, they are better able to unite when a joint parental stand is required, as it often is during their child's adolescence. A teenager may exploit ignorance and differences between the two households, playing one parent against the other to gain freedoms that would be prohibited by both, if both only knew. Ex-partners must be able to communicate directly in order to get the straight story about what is really happening. Should they depend on the teenager's self-serving account, they are liable to be led astray.

Divorce is a declaration of independence. Ending marriage, the partners agree to live apart. Pushing the ex-spouse away is a necessity for this separation to become established. In the best of all possible circumstances, what divorced parents can communicate to their children is the following message: "Although we can't live happily in marriage as partners, we can still work cooperatively together as your parents, and we shall."

35

~~~~~~

MAINTAINING COOPERATION

DEALING WITH DIFFERENCES AFTER DIVORCE

Whatever personality and preference differences divided the marriage, they tend to grow more pronounced after divorce when each partner is freed to pursue life on his and her own individual terms. Now there is no concern about giving offense by following inclinations and indulging habits the ex-partner doesn't like. Freedom apart increases diversity between former partners, sometimes requiring tolerance from them both when communication and cooperation between them as parents is required for their children.

These lifestyle differences, unless clearly harmful to children by creating danger from neglect or abuse, need to be respected, not contested. Personal dissimilarities will create differences in parenting, and that's okay. The two households do not have to be entirely consistent. Engaging in personal criticism after divorce presumes more influence than either parent now has the right to claim. Neither of them has to govern their separate lives out of consideration for the other anymore; some parenting responsibility is all they share. Where consistency is helpful, like supervising regular exercises to remediate a child's special need, parents can discuss to what degree this can be practically accomplished.

Henceforth, it is not beneficial for one parent to complain about a difference in the other to children who feel conflicted when this occurs. It is better to acknowledge and explain the increased diversity to the children. "You will live somewhat differently with each of us, because now we live more differently from each other. This doesn't mean that one way is right and the other is wrong. However, you will have to learn to adjust to these differences as you go back and forth between the two households."

Beyond respecting *lifestyle differences*, however, there are differences that can arise over managing visitation and providing child support. These are *contractual differences*, and respect alone will not resolve them. Negotiation and compromise are demanded. For example, when a child enters adolescence and his or her social world becomes of primary importance, the traditional schedule of visitation may no longer work as easily as before. Now it competes with the teenager's growing social commitments, and the son or daughter frequently needs to make adjustments. This alteration in their child needs to be discussed between the parents. Otherwise, the noncustodial parent may feel rejected or may wrongfully suspect the custodial parent of withholding the teenager from visitation. In addition, the teenager and the noncustodial parent need to negotiate a more flexible schedule of visitation that accommodates the social change that growth has caused. To maintain adequate continuity of contact between more irregular visits, noncustodial parents can increase telephone and written communication. They can schedule more brief contacts between less frequent extended visits. And they can encourage the teenager to bring a friend along on the next visitation.

The initial divorce decree is only that, a *first agreement*. Informally, and perhaps formally, it may need to be modified as children grow and become more expensive to support. What matters most is the process parents use to redefine this agreement as change takes place. Each partner needs to give some to get some; each must be willing to *compromise*. In one sense, compromise is a losing proposition. It means getting less than 100 percent of what each party would ideally like. The benefit of compromise, however, is that it puts the ongoing well-being of the relationship first, with each partner subordinating some self-interest to the larger interest they both share: parenting the children whom they love. To become adversarial with each other only polarizes the relationship, creating tensions and oppositions that retard cooperation and impact on the children.

When a hard difference arises, like the custodial parent wanting an increase in child support that the noncustodial parent resists, and the two are unable to reach a compromise, they should try mediation before going to litigation. Mediation invites a third party into the relationship to help the couple negotiate a difficult difference they cannot resolve by themselves. Through a process in which the sensitivities of each are respected, the mediator helps both parties reach an agreement neither may entirely like, but both are willing to accept. A mediated agreement allows them to continue to maintain a working cooperation, and not be alienated by unresolved conflict.

The reality is, divorce does not end all the problems between a husband and wife. They still remain "married" as a father and mother. Therefore, after divorce, they must try to keep their relationship communicative and cooperative for the sake of the children.

36

〰〰〰〰〰〰〰〰〰〰〰〰〰〰〰〰〰〰〰〰〰〰〰〰〰〰〰〰〰〰〰〰〰〰〰〰〰〰〰

LETTING GRIEVANCE GO

KEEPING CLEAR OF RESENTMENT

Divorce requires three separations in order to become complete. Legally, the marriage must be dissolved. Socially, the partners must agree to live apart. Emotionally, they must let go any longing to get back with or back at one another. It is this last separation that usually takes longest, particularly getting over injuries received during the marriage that can linger as resentments after divorce.

Strong positive or negative feelings for the ex-spouse beyond divorce betray an attachment that custodial parents can ill afford. Not only does this holding on to the past drain precious energy from the present, it slows growth of their new independence by tying them to the old relationship. They are still married in regret or anger. Only by mourning the loss of the loved one, or by accepting the reality of marital hurt, can they freely grow forward. By expressing and exploring their feelings with family, friends, or helpers, they can at last come to terms of acceptance with their pain. Communication can heal hurtful experience.

Unhappily, resolving old grievances at the ex-spouse does not prevent new ones from arising once the divorce is done. For example, custodial parents may resent the good and easy time their ex-spouse and the children have together on visitation. Beforehand, the children get excited, during visitation they have nonstop fun, and returning home they are so grateful for everything the noncustodial parent did to entertain and make them happy. How can custodial parents compete with this performance? They can't. By comparison, home seems dull and ordinary, boring and routine.

To custodial parents, who feel overworked and under-valued, this comparison feels unfair. Who does the drudgery of daily supervision? Who keeps the home stocked and supplied? Who asserts demands, defends limits, enforces rules, and disciplines violations? Who settles fights, soothes upsets, attends sickness, and solves problems? Who bears constant responsibility for the children's care? Where are the thanks for doing all this? Nowhere. Custodial parents either feel taken for granted by their children, or blamed for being moody when they're tired. It feels like a double standard, and it is. Although the children expect less from the noncustodial parent, they appreciate that occasional parent more. Although they expect much more from the custodial parent, they seem to appreciate that constant parenting far less.

Before custodial parents give into this resentment, however, they might want to consider this apparent inequity from another perspective. In terms of the children's trust and openness, their relationships with the two parents can be very different. Between children and their noncustodial parent there is sometimes something missing: authenticity. Wanting so much to make their visit a success, the special effort to please each other that children and their noncustodial parent make often gets in the way of expressing hard feelings that normally arise. Neither adult nor children, for example, may feel comfortable expressing anger or dissatisfaction with the other, or making demands that would spoil their limited time together. This is often a "best behavior" relationship on both sides, neither party wanting to disappoint the other or arouse their disapproval. For this reason, some degree of authenticity is sacrificed for the sake of harmony. When full intimacy is restrained, children and the noncustodial parent often come away from visitation feeling mixed. They had a good time, and yet feel dissatisfied because they did not connect as completely as both longed to do.

In one way it is true that the noncustodial parent gets the best behavior from the children, and the custodial parent gets the worst. But on a deeper level, this statement can be false. With their custodial mother or father, the children have an open enough relationship to risk sharing their worst sides, unafraid that by doing so they will jeopardize their standing with the resident parent. Although being taken for granted can be irritating at times, custodial parents can also treat this assumption as a compliment and statement of trust. The children are implying: "Because you are always here, and because you will always love and accept us, we don't have to worry about our bad moods or misbehavior driving you away. Because we live together, we don't have to act like it's a visit. We can just relax and be ourselves."

What custodial parents get is usually an honest mix of good and bad from their children, whereas their ex-spouse must often make do mostly with the good.

37

VISITATION ADJUSTMENTS

THE TRANSITION BETWEEN SEPARATE HOMES

No matter how well managed, visitation can still be a complicated arrangement for divorced parents and their child. Understand some of these complexities and the adjustments can be eased.

When approaching visitation, remember differences. It was irreconcilable differences between each partner's ways and wants that caused the marriage to dissolve. After divorce, those incompatibilities that initially drove the couple apart usually grow more pronounced, becoming evident in the different lifestyles that the former partners lead, and the different households that they run. Because visitation requires children to bridge these differences, going back and forth takes getting used to. The transition is complicated. It requires more than simply walking out of one door and in through another. Children must let go of one family frame of reference and then reengage with another.

Management of their children's reentry into the home is one of the most complex tasks custodial parents have to master. Pressures of getting back together and possibilities for misunderstanding, create an increased vulnerability to hurt and conflict.

Consider the simple problem of *timing*. A custodial parent, happy to see the children after a weekend, holiday, or vacation separation, wants an affectionate and communicative reunion. One child, however, remains distant and cool, only wanting to be left alone. The custodial parent thinks: "Why am I being treated this way? Haven't I been missed at all? Isn't the child glad to be home?"

The answer to the last two questions is "yes." The child *has* missed the custodial parent and *is* glad to be home. He or she has not yet let go of the visit with the other parent, however, and still wants to reflect on the memory of their being together. Thus preoccupied, the child acts removed and unresponsive, wanting time to emotionally close out the visit. He or she loves the custodial parent, but is not ready to reconnect and open up just yet.

In this situation, custodial parents are well advised, after communicating welcome, to give the child privacy and space. Rather than treat this aloofness as rejection, respect it for what it really is—a period of difficult adjustment for which the child needs some time alone.

This strategy is even more important after a bad visit, when the child's expectations were disappointed or some troublesome incident occurred. In either case, the child may have avoided speaking up, not wanting to make a disagreeable situation worse. As soon as he or she returns home, however, out come the injured feelings. The unhappy child picks on a sibling or at the custodial parent, looking for a fight to get that pent up anger out.

Again, the custodial parent needs not to take this treatment personally. Instead, say to the child: "It sounds like you may have had a hard visit. Take some time alone to settle down, then we can talk about what happened if you like." Over the course of many visitations, not every one will go well. When they don't, the child may bring bad feelings home. Acting them out in anger, however, although understandable, is not acceptable. The child must learn to talk them out in such a way that they bring relief without inflicting harm to others. His or her custodial parent is happy to be a sympathetic listener, but not a whipping post.

Another complexity of visitation can arise from different degrees of freedom between the two households. Returning children may start pressuring the custodial parent to retract certain demands and grant certain permissions because that's how things were done at the other home. "Well they let me do this, and they never made me do that!" goes the comparison. Because visiting children tend to be given more special allowances than resident children, the child may be telling the truth.

Custodial parents, however, need to adhere to the family structure they have created, firmly reasserting the rules and routines that govern their household. As a consequence of the child pushing for change, and the custodial parent enforcing the status quo, some conflict may occur immediately following reentry from a visitation. Fortunately, after some initial testing and complaint, children usually accept that they are back home where "business as usual" applies. Deep down they knew they weren't really going to change their custodial parent. They just felt compelled to try.

Probably the most painful reentries occur when divorce is unreconciled and parents remain actively embittered toward each other. In this unforgiving circumstance, the child cannot act pleased to see one parent without offending the other. Constant pressure to take sides is increased by visitation when parents treat leaving their home as a betrayal of loyalty, as though the child were going to take up residence in the enemy's camp. In either household, the child may feel resentment and hear slander from one parent toward the other. One can sympathize with the weary twelve-year-old who angrily declared: "Sometimes I wish I could divorce both of them and just live alone!"

It takes parents who have emotionally divorced to honestly support the child's contact with each other, blessing the child's passage back and forth between two homes.

38

▲▲

HARD STANDS

OPPOSING THE NONCUSTODIAL PARENT
FOR THE CHILD'S WELL-BEING

Circumstances can arise when custodial parents must act for their child's best interest in ways their ex-spouse may not like. In the process, anger can be provoked and conflict created, with custodial parents taking stands that the ex-spouse may consider offensive and unjust.

What kinds of stands? The most common two are for *child safety* and for *child support*. In both instances, custodial parents must look out for the child's welfare by monitoring treatment while on visitation and by assessing ongoing financial needs at home.

Taking issue with the noncustodial parent's conduct is not easy when that former partner feels that what happens during visitation is none of the custodial parent's business. Nor is it any easier to take issue with monetary contribution when the former partner believes that the initial settlement for child support should remain the final one. *The noncustodial parent is wrong on both counts.*

Custodial parents have ongoing responsibility for evaluating what occurs on visitation, and for ensuring the child's adequate support at home. Avoiding advocacy for their child out of fear that the noncustodial parent might be offended gives that former partner's displeasure extortionate power. "I'd rather put up with problems than speak up and get my ex upset." By such statements of appeasement, custodial parents may be slighting their child's basic needs or condoning the child getting hurt. It can take courage to confront unpleasant issues with an angry ex-spouse.

Child Safety

Custodial parents need to speak up to their ex-spouse about visitation concerns that the child only feels secure voicing at home. Consider safety first. Suppose that when describing visitation, the child confides to the custodial parent one of the following kinds of reservations:

- "I'm left alone too much."
- "I'm given more responsibility than I know how to handle."
- "I get hurt by how I'm treated."
- "I get punished too hard."
- "I'm frightened about what might happen."
- "I don't trust that I'll be taken care of."
- "Sometimes I dread going."
- "Sometimes I wish I didn't have to go back."

These kinds of statements must be taken seriously. Custodial parents should first listen and then ask the child to *specify* what is happening or not happening to cause these feelings. After telling the child what they are going to do, custodial parents must then inform the noncustodial parent about conduct and circumstances that are causing the child to feel unsafe. These concerns should be expressed in terms of *reported* behaviors that happen and *reported* situations that occur. Although the noncustodial parent may respond with information that modifies the child's report, it is with the child's *feelings* that the custodial parent is most concerned. The custodial parent is not interested in making accusations against the ex-spouse, but is wanting to help make visitation feel as comfortable as possible for the child. To this end, the custodial parent is giving the noncustodial parent information that may be useful in making visitation a more positive experience. The custodial parent needs to send his or her ex-spouse this message: "I want you to know that I value your time with our child and want that time to be beneficial to you both. This is why I am sharing this information with you now." Approached in this supportive manner, in many cases the noncustodial parent will make modifications that improve the quality of visitation.

Where the noncustodial parent reacts in denial, however, stubbornly refusing to admit visitation is causing distress or risking injury, custodial parents may have to take a protective stand. They may need to resort to some child protective agent like a family law attorney or to some child protective agency, like Domestic Services or Child Welfare, in order to stop continuing suffering or to prevent possible injury. Sometimes just knowing outside officials have been notified is enough to cause the noncustodial parent to behave more responsibly.

To place the child in visitation at the effect of neglect, abuse, alcoholism, drug addiction, recklessness, violence, or other danger, is not simply a matter of irresponsible parenting by the noncustodial parent. It is equally irresponsible for the custodial parent to knowingly send the child into harm's way.

Child Support

Being asked to raise existing child support payments often affronts noncustodial parents. They feel they are already giving enough. Besides, if they raise their contribution, they don't get any more benefit in return. If remarried, their new spouse may resent this additional drain on resources he or she feels should be devoted to the new family, not the old.

In making this request, the custodial parent is best served by documenting the existing need. Present the following:

1. The schedule of basic expenses required to support the child at the time of divorce
2. A revision of these expenses based on how they have increased as the child has grown older and inflation has raised the cost of living
3. An addition of special unanticipated expenses that have arisen since the original settlement
4. A statement of how the custodial parent has had to spend more on the child too

A request to raise child support is evidence that the custodial parent is also having to contribute more than before. All he or she is really asking is for the ex-spouse to share in this increase.

Just as parental marriage is never ended by divorce, with ex-partners still connected through their children, so divorce is never finished until the last child reaches the age of self-support. When financial dependency between the former marriage partners is over, then each is finally free of legal obligation to the other.

39

‸‸‸

WHEN A MARRIAGE PARTNER DIES

MOURNING THE LOSS

D ivorce is a matter of choice for at least one partner; death of a partner is not elective. Divorce does not necessarily deprive children of ever seeing the other parent again; death closes that possibility forever. Conflict and estrangement tend to characterize the marriage preceding divorce; caring and caretaking are more often the rule leading up to a partner's death.

For a widowed mother or father, the entry into single parenthood is often traumatic. There is the unwelcome loss of a partner for one's self and of a parent for the children. Mourning both losses must be honored while reorganizing the family to meet a host of unexpected demands. Although difficult to address, these practical demands for readjustment are actually supportive. They divert some attention away from pain into solving problems, and they dictate necessary actions for carrying on. Responsibility for children requires that widowed parents maintain forward momentum through the crisis that death has created.

What about grieving? Should widowed parents share personal grief with the children or toughen up, be strong, and not increase the children's sorrow by expressing sorrow of their own? The answer is to share parental pain, but to do so within limits. Children learn how to cope with life's adversities by watching the example of their parents. Thus, a time for mourning is a time to model for the children how mourning is done—by letting in, letting out, and gradually letting go of the hurt that loss has caused. A parent who conceals pain to protect the children may unwittingly teach covering up. The children may become discouraged from acknowledging, expressing, and releasing pain of their own.

At the other extreme, a stricken father or mother who depends upon children for his or her sole emotional support can burden them too heavily. They may sacrifice their own bereavement needs to satisfy those of the unhappy parent. Between these two alternatives lies a middle way. The widowed parent, having found outside support for heavy grieving, can helpfully share with children some of the many losses that this loss from death has personally created.

Consider seven different kinds of losses that death of spouse and parent can create.

1. There is a loss of *understanding*. A change like death takes the survivors from a known into an unknown situation. Life has become uncertain. What will happen to them now? The emotional consequence of confronting this ignorance is anxiety. Neither the widowed parent nor the children yet understand how they can cope with what's ahead. They feel at a loss and they are. As time passes, however, knowledge from experience is gained and worry from ignorance becomes reduced. From every loss to be mourned, there is growth to be gained. After the loss of understanding, new knowledge is acquired to supplement the old.

2. There is a loss of *connection*. A primary relationship has been severed. The survivor's traditional definition

of family is gone forever. From this rending loss, grief naturally flows. The single parent and children miss the partner or parent whom they had. Longing and loneliness beget much pain. It takes crying time for recovery to occur. Grieving helps heal the hurt. Then fresh connections must be forged. Over time, filling the emptiness requires creating new bonds of love.

3. There is a loss of *power*. Forces beyond the control of the single parent and children, and against their hearts' desire, have taken the husband or wife, father or mother away. In response, they may feel like a helpless victim. Angry at first at fate for treating them unfairly, single parents may then experience anger at the loved one. The deceased spouse has left them bereft of support, burdened by responsibilities, and beset by hardships, having to cope and carry on alone. Children may rage as well, angry from feeling abandoned by the dead parent. In time, strength from coping gradually grows. As a sense of control is restored, anger from the loss of power subsides.

4. There is a loss of *acceptance*. To become widowed, fatherless, or motherless, is to become different from how one was, how many others are, and how one wishes to be. What difference will this difference make? Unwanted differences tend to be rejected. For this reason, the widowed parent and children may go through a period of self-rejection. Because something bad has happened to them, maybe this means they are being punished. Maybe they did wrong or something is wrong with them. Social rejection can also occur. Other people, out of their own fear of dying, may shy away from a family visited by death. Widowed parents and their children, however, grow more tolerant of the reality of death in life, and become more accepting of

145

leading lives that, through no failing of their own, have been marked by a loved one's death.

5. There is a loss of *confidence.* So much was taken care of by the partner and parent who has died. The family depended on him or her in so many ways. Now who will provide and caretake in that person's stead? Can those functions be replaced by the survivors? Can other members of the family learn to do what was done for them? Adequacy is questioned and doubts are raised. However, at necessity's insistence, and in service of survival, new competencies are learned, and thus, lost confidence becomes regained.

6. There is a loss of *identity.* To lose a spouse or parent is to have part of one's personal and social identity taken away. By association, caring, and dependency, those loved become intimately linked to one's sense of who one is. Feeling momentarily diminished without the loved one's presence, deprived of the old role in that relationship, the single parent and children can go through a period of confusion about their definition. Who are they now without the old connection? The answer is to be found in a growing sense of clarity. In time, they discover a new sense of individuality independent of the partner or parent who has been lost.

7. There is a loss of *faith.* When death removes a loved one from the family, painful questions can be raised about the meaning and justice of life. How can such a bad thing happen to good people? And if it can, then what does this say about the higher power in which they have invested their belief? Personal tragedy shakes faith, tests it, and in time allows the single parent and children to reaffirm that faith on a

deeper level. They come to understand that personal misfortune is part of human life.

Mourning death means acknowledging and expressing loss on many levels—loss of understanding, of connecting, of power, of acceptance, of confidence, of identity, and of faith, among others. As widowed parents share the different losses that they feel, describing the emotions that are touched, children are given permission to confront losses of their own. They are encouraged to begin the mourning process for themselves.

Readiness to mourn will vary among children. Some begin right away to inventory their losses. Other children delay the experience of pain by denying feelings, or by acting them out through aggression (hostility), regression (insecurity), or depression (helplessness). When acting out occurs, single parents need to encourage direct expression by talking out emotions that actions may conceal. Otherwise, acting out may be taken at face value. In school, for example, bereaved children can get punished for angry misbehavior, yet their underlying suffering is ignored. Enlisting the help of a school counselor can sometimes help a child get emotionally unstuck. For example, when a child is referred from class after another tantrum, he or she anticipates a lecture. Instead, the counselor asks: "Can you tell me what you're feeling when you act that way?" Instead of arguing about what really happened and whose fault it was, the counselor and the child begin to explore the emotion that acting out was covering up.

Hard as it is to imagine when the effects of death still feel traumatic, this tragedy will yield surviving family members some *gifts of adversity* in the form of growth that otherwise would not have occurred. What does not defeat them, makes them stronger. The other side of loss is freedom. There will be some *freedom for* new opportunities. There will be some *freedom from* old restraints.

The process of recovery, however, is not quickly accomplished. Widowed parents need to be persistent in their efforts and patient with their headway. Allow two years for the major adjustment to be accomplished. Pause every few months to inventory the problems that still linger, and to appreciate the progress that is arduously being made.

In many larger communities there are bereavement groups that provide support not only for the widowed parent, but for children as well. These groups can be located by calling the local or state mental health association, the public schools, hospitals, or churches. Bereavement groups teach a process through which established stages of grief can be addressed in an empathetic setting that allows emotion to be safely expressed.

40

~~~~~~

HEALING THE LONELINESS

RECONNECTING THE BROKEN BONDS OF CARING

When death of a partner leads a person into single parenthood, a journey into loneliness has begun. The widowed parent longs for the union that has been lost, and dreads a future raising children all alone. To grow beyond loneliness, it helps to understand what "lonely" is, and how to alleviate its pain.

Loneliness is rooted in all caring relationships for two opposing reasons. People want sufficient closeness to maintain a fulfilling connection with each other, but they also want enough separation to preserve personal freedom and identity. With too much separation, people long for time together, becoming lonely from feeling out of touch with each other. With too much closeness, people long for time apart, becoming lonely from feeling out of touch with themselves. Because loneliness can arise from feeling alone too much or too little, relationships require a constant balancing of these needs for closeness and separation.

By its final nature, widowhood first creates loneliness from terminal separation. Surviving partners miss the marital companionship that has been lost. By its stressful nature, widowhood then creates loneliness for single parents from being too busy to have time just for themselves. Overwhelmed by job and household demands and child care responsibilities, they miss the gift of solitude. Both changes cause them to feel lonely. Supportive company helps keep the widowed parent from feeling too isolated. Making time for privacy creates the opportunity for being beneficially alone.

Human loneliness is a universal affliction with common origins. It arises in relationships when one or more of three caring connections are missing, injured, or broken:

1. When caring *from* valued others is diminished or lost, a person can feel lonely. "My spouse isn't there to care for me any longer."
2. When caring *for* valued others is diminished or lost, a person can feel lonely. "I don't have a partner to give my love to any more."
3. When *sense of oneself* is diminished as a function of loss, a person can feel lonely. "I feel lessened as a person by the death of my spouse."

By breaking each connection, widowhood creates loneliness on all three counts.

The primary connection to repair is the most intimate: restoration of one's sense of self. When over many years of marriage, through dependence and mutuality, couples come to share a common sense of identity, the death of a partner can leave an enormous void. "I have lost my other half" is how some widowed parents will describe it "and I don't feel whole any more." Feeling empty is one way of feeling lonely. To fill themselves back up takes solitary time for reflection and dedicated time pursuing interests, mining self-knowledge, and affirming self-worth. They need to convince themselves that they can eventually feel complete and happy without the other person being present in their life.

The second connection to repair is caring for others because, unlike caring from others, it is a connection widowed parents can control. By reaching out to family for support, to friends for companionship, even to strangers through volunteer helping, initiative is exercised that keeps caring alive and creates meaningful contact with others. The message widowed parents send themselves through reaching out is vital. "Relationships still matter. I do not have to be alone." When losing a partner causes the widowed parent to withdraw from other people, grief and isolation can combine to encourage depression and despair. The task of early widowhood is to mourn the dead while remaining connected to the living.

Once widowed, however, what is to be done with the love and attention formerly given the departed spouse? Children, although an obvious choice, are not the only answer, by giving all that love to them. They cannot substitute for adult companionship, nor should they try. Yet the widowed parent is still too emotionally wed to consider dating. Some loneliness must be endured, in missing an adult intimacy that cannot soon be replaced. Although disinclined by grief to socialize, perhaps feeling awkward as a single person, widowed parents need to force themselves out into company, going through the motions to actively maintain connections so that social isolation does not compound existing pain.

The third connection to repair is the most difficult: loneliness created when death has cost the loss of the person whose caring mattered most of all. Partly valued and partly taken for granted, this relationship, and the daily attentions and responses that went with it, is missed in a host of little ways, each one a painful reminder of the larger loss.

The natural state of feeling bereft and focusing inward cannot only discourage reaching out, it can discourage overtures of caring coming in. Push these invitations away often enough and others, feeling their offers of concern rejected, may decide to leave the widowed parent alone. It is hard to be socially receptive when preoccupied with grief, but that receptivity is as necessary as an initiative for reaching out.

When someone calls or visits to see how everything is going, or invites the family over there, it may feel like too much effort to respond. The widowed parent may feel: "I don't have the social energy to give." Making the effort, however, is worthwhile because maintaining old relationships and creating new ones is what ultimately recovers both the surviving parent and the children from loneliness that death has caused.

41

^^

COMMEMORATION

KEEPING THE LOVED ONE'S MEMORY ALIVE

To make peace with a significant loss requires mourning more than once. The pain must be revisited time and again. Each repetition allows the expression of further grief and encourages more understanding of how one's life has been affected.

As loss is reexperienced on subsequent occasions, over days and weeks and months and years, a transformation gradually occurs. Remembrance of the death feels less painful and recollection of the person lost becomes more affirming. Loss only hurts, however, if what is lost has value. In some painful family situations, the death of a troubled or destructive parent and partner may come as a relief. In many others, however, there is a sincere and heartfelt sense of loss.

In early mourning, most feeling focuses on what is missed. In later mourning, focus shifts to appreciate the departed spouse or parent, to be grateful for gifts he or she left behind. Without denying difficulties that this person may have caused, these gifts become important to enumerate:

- There are the positive qualities the person represented.
- There are the good times that were had together.
- There are contributions the person made to the lives of other family members.
- There are lessons about living that continue to instruct and to inspire.

Early mourning is marked by grieving and support. Later mourning is marked by positive recollection and *storytelling* about what the deceased partner or parent did and said. This oral history, its telling and retelling, is an extremely important part of the mourning process because it fixes the dead person in the collective memory of the family. As that memory is passed down from one generation to the next, those who come after feel connected to those who went before.

During the first one to two years after the death, it is valuable for the surviving parent to take some reflective and expressive time with each child to recall the parent who has died, and to encourage the child's feelings out. Like reopening a wound to drain infection so it can heal clean, these talks create an opportunity for the child to bring back up, and go back through, how the death felt and what it is coming to mean.

Like loops in time, holidays, birthdays, traditional observances, and anniversary events tend to invoke similar occasions in the past when the dead was among the living. Memories are stimulated and feelings are stirred. There may be tears from what is missed, some laughter at what is remembered, and some beloved stories told again that have been told before.

Commemoration is an act of healing. It unites everyone around a common loss, creating a bond of shared history. It transforms grief into appreciation for the relationship that once upon a time they shared together.

42

‹‹

GETTING DOWN TO BASICS

MAKING ENDS MEET

Social attitudes affect the treatment that one receives. Thus, the widowed single parent gets sympathy for experiencing a tragic loss. The divorced single parent is granted understanding, because so many marriages fail to last. The abandoned single-parent mother, however, is given little sympathy in our society, and much less support. Instead, not only must she struggle for survival of her family, but she is frequently censured for the dire economic circumstances in which she has been left. Society seems to forgive and forget the father, blame the mother, and begrudge helping the financially vulnerable family, thereby penalizing the innocent child.

The abandoned single parent may be demeaned for claiming the minimal public assistance she oftentimes desperately needs, and to which she is by law entitled. A double standard prevails. If mothers abandoned their children as readily as many fathers, then society would be providing for a host of deserted children. Although mothers are expected to honor their biological commitment, fathers are given permission to leave that responsibility behind.

For most abandoned single-parent mothers, unrelenting economic hardship is the everyday reality with which they must contend. Often with no child support from absent fathers, they must rely on what they can earn, in many cases at minimum wage jobs with no benefits. Their families can sometimes help out, and as long as they remain financially eligible there may be social services to provide some support. If they are receiving public assistance (family stipend, housing allowance, food stamps, medical aid, child care, or educational grants), making a little more money can mean a loss of benefits, worsening the situation they were trying to better. It is a hard contradiction to accept: the price of getting ahead is giving up crucial support.

For young women who get pregnant during junior high or high school, it becomes all the more difficult and all the more important for them to graduate. At stake is future employability and educational opportunity, both of which materially affect their potential to support themselves and the child later on.

The decision to remain in school, however, can be difficult to make. Arrangements must be found for day care and that costs money, unless a family member or friend steps in to help. Even then, after-school baby care ties the young mother down at an age when going out with friends and having fun is what life is supposed to be about. Early motherhood can bring an early end to adolescence. Life gets serious sooner than expected. Social freedom must be given up and adult responsibilities assumed. A rite of passage has taken place. The young woman is no longer a child; she is a parent. Now she must think for two instead of one.

Because there is a lot to think about, it helps to have a more experienced adult (relative or friend, teacher at school or nurse at the clinic, counselor or social worker) to give advice, to assist in planning, and to help problem solve. There is so much to figure out: child care, health care, housing, food, clothing, employment, education, managing time, money, and transportation. How is the young mother going to put all these pieces of the puzzle in place? She needs to find a *mentor* she can trust.

Although the amount of federal and state support for low-income, single-parent mothers was never very high, it is getting lower. As entitlements are cut back, these vulnerable families are placed more at social risk. Some assistance, however, is still available. The kind and amount of support vary with geographical location and individual circumstance. The young abandoned mother needs to find out from her local or state department of human services what program help is offered in her area. This means learning eligibility requirements. It also means being willing to go through application procedures that can feel confusing, impersonal, uncaring, or even punitive. Ignorance may be answered with impatience. Treatment may feel insulting. Having the company of a friend or family member on these occasions can discourage mistreatment by making public what would otherwise be a private encounter.

What to remember is that there is no shame in being in need, and that one is entitled to public assistance established by law. At all levels, this country is a welfare society—special interests get tax breaks, farmers get subsidies, failing businesses are bailed out, emergency relief is given to victims of disaster, and social support is provided to those who struggle for survival against poverty.

Then there is the father. Just because the woman is left with the child doesn't mean that she should bear total parenting responsibility, and the man none. At the hospital, paternity can be made a matter of public record. If denied, it can be verified by testing. Child support obligation can be claimed. By asserting this expectation of support, the mother lets the father know that he has ongoing responsibility as well as she. She is entitled to his support, and by becoming familiar with the laws of her state, through the agencies empowered to carry them out, she can pursue the contribution that she and her child deserve. Legal steps can be taken to garnish the father's wages for support.

As for relationships with other men, abandoned single-parent mothers must beware that their longing for a committed relationship is not exploited by seductive promises that won't be kept. In addition, sexual relations should be planned to provide protection against unwanted pregnancy and life-threatening disease.

43

~~~~~~

KEEPING ON KEEPING ON

MANAGING MOTIVATION

What older abandoned mothers soon discover is the fragile nature of family security when constant economic pressure is a fact of daily life. When one pillar of survival is momentarily shaken, the entire structure can be threatened with collapse. A day care arrangement that fails or a sick child who requires a mother to stay home, can jeopardize a job with no tolerance for emergencies or allowance for leave. Even positive changes can prove costly. Moving to a more affordable space can mean moving children into yet one more school where they must learn to start all over again. One hardship quickly creates another.

Life can become crisis driven, with continual upheaval causing ongoing stress. In these circumstances, how can the abandoned mother keep herself motivated? Three questions can be helpful to ask:

1. "What have I accomplished today?"
2. "What strengths do my accomplishments reflect?"
3. "How am I working to improve the lives of my child and myself?"

The first question, "What have I accomplished today?" may not seem worth asking when the automatic answer is:

"Nothing, I just survived." This response is self-defeating and wrong. Survival beats giving up. It means effort has been made. It means her actions have succeeded in keeping the hard-pressed family still afloat. This effort and this outcome need to be acknowledged. She has not done "nothing." She has done a lot. Evidence for this accomplishment can be gathered by itemizing some of the basic steps she took to get herself and the children through another challenging day. Holding one's own against a constant current of hardship is an achievement. She needs to give herself recognition for all she does.

The second question, "What strengths do my accomplishments reflect?" requires some thought. What does it take to keep on keeping on? Required are qualities that confronting daily hardship can confer: commitment, stamina, courage, tenacity, sacrifice, resourcefulness, and determination, to name a few. And because what parents primarily give to their children is who and how they are, these qualities model strengths that children can acquire from their mother's example. These traits, and the character they build, become the gifts of adversity that one has the right and responsibility to claim. Owning them is an act of self-respect.

The third question, "How am I working to improve the lives of myself and my child?" anchors the mother to a future worth striving for. Set goals and possibilities are created. Pursue those possibilities and progress can be made. Make progress and hope is nourished, overcoming the discouragement of daily struggle. It is hard to feel helpless and downcast when actively pursuing goals.

Responsibility for her children's future can cause a mother to focus more clearly on her own, because what happens for them depends a lot on what happens for her. "If I want something better for my kids, I'm going to have to do something better for myself." If she can improve her situation educationally and occupationally, she can increase the likelihood of improving theirs.

Self-support is not only an economic concern, it is a motivational one. The abandoned single mother must keep her self-esteem and momentum up when daily difficulty and social prejudice are pushing her down.

44

^^

WATCHING EDUCATION CAREFULLY

KEEPING THE CLASSROOM EXPERIENCE POSITIVE

The last problem abandoned mothers need, in addition to everything else they must cope with, is for a son or daughter to begin having problems at school. If the teacher grows increasingly unhappy with the child's behavior, the child may have to experience the force of that unhappiness each day. The outcome can be sad to see.

How children are responded to in class can affect how they respond to themselves. Continually treated negatively by the teacher at school, they can come home feeling bad about who and how they are. When this occurs, the mother needs to notice and take action right away.

The longer that children remain a problem for one teacher, the more likely that they will be treated as a problem by other teachers later on. Why? Because standing with one teacher can affect standing with the next, with the first teacher warning others to watch out for a certain difficult child who is coming their way. Children are not free to establish a new reputation in the next grade when their old reputation has preceded them. Slander sets negative expectations that may self-fulfill by provoking a negative response from the child.

When their child starts experiencing trouble with a teacher at school, single mothers have three tasks:

1. Understand why school demands more adjustment from some children than others.
2. Communicate with the teacher and specify the nature of the child's problems.
3. Coach the child on how he or she has the power to change the teacher's behavior from negative to positive.

A teacher is required to manage a large group of children, not simply to work with one child at a time. Because of the teacher's collective responsibility, the major burden is on each child to adjust to how that class is being conducted. It is not the other way around—school does not tailor the classroom to the needs of each individual child.

Ease of adjustment for the child depends a lot on how closely the classroom experience resembles experience at home. The child's adjustment to school tends to go smoothly if the following factors are met:

- The teacher's norms for acceptable behavior are similar to what is expected at home.
- The necessary skills for adequate performance have been learned at home.
- The content of what is being taught is already familiar from home.

The child is comfortable with the demands of the teacher, the teacher is comfortable with the readiness of the child, and the relationship works well for them both. This child enters school at a social advantage.

Conversely, if the teacher's norms and expectations, curriculum and methods, and rules and directions are mostly unfamiliar to a child, he or she can get off to a rocky start. By not immediately conforming to expectations, comprehending content, and complying with rules, the child can test a teacher's patience. For persistently not fitting in, not going along, and not understanding, the child can get criticized. If punishment is added to criticism, the child can become more negatively disposed to school, acting in ways that the teacher considers a problem. Then a cycle is created that can be difficult to break. The harder the child is for the teacher to instruct, the harder that teacher can be on that child, and the more resistant the child may become in return.

This cycle, however, can be broken. To begin with, the mother needs to find out what adjustments are most difficult for her child. She can do this by asking what is hardest to get used to at school in general, and in class in particular. "Sitting at the back of the class, I can't concentrate on what the teacher is saying because of all the other students doing stuff in front of me. Then I get punished for not paying attention." In getting this information, the mother is also allowing the child to give voice to whatever frustrations are attached to these hardships. She is encouraging the expression of feelings that may have been held in, built up, and acted out in class.

Equipped with the child's information, the mother can then communicate with the teacher to find out what difficulty he or she is experiencing with the child. If the teacher makes generalized complaints by saying that the child is "disrespectful," "unmanageable," or "uncooperative," the mother needs to specify these abstract labels to make them useful. What is the child doing or not doing to cause the teacher to use the label "disrespectful?" The teacher explains: when the student takes without asking and interrupts without waiting to be called on, the teacher considers these actions "disrespectful." Now the mother has some specific behaviors that she can discuss with her child.

She is trying to provide the teacher with information about specific adjustments that are hard for the child, and to provide the child with information about specific behaviors that are hard for the teacher. The mother wants to build a basis for concrete understanding between them. She wants to keep the strained relationship free from evaluative labels so that each party can concentrate on making specific changes to better get along.

Finally, the mother can work with her child to improve the relationship with the teacher. She can tell the child that he or she has the power to change the teacher from someone "mean" (mostly acting negative) into someone "nice" (mostly acting positive). How is this magic to be accomplished? Choices can control consequences. Tell the child that if he or she will do exactly what the mother says for three days, the teacher will change in ways the child will like.

Then the mother explains to the child about three basic teacher needs with students: to be liked, to be in control, and to be successful. Satisfy those needs and the teacher will like you; frustrate those needs and the teacher will not. Consider:

- How can the child communicate *liking* to the teacher? Maybe by greeting the teacher, maybe by smiling at the teacher, or maybe by offering to help the teacher.
- How can the child act like the teacher is in *control*? Maybe by changing tasks when the teacher says to, maybe by not speaking out until called on, or maybe by remembering not to run down the hall.
- How can the child help the teacher feel *successful*? Maybe by completing class work and homework on time, maybe by carefully following instructions, or maybe by asking for help when the child does not understand.

Give most teachers three days with a "problem" student who starts to satisfy their basic needs, and teacher attitude tends to become more positive. As the teacher starts feeling better about the student, he or she begins treating the student better. As the student begins to be treated better, he or she begins to have a better sense of self, and feels encouraged to continue acting better in response. Seeing these improvements, the single mother feels better about how her child is doing in school.

QUESTIONS AND ANSWERS

Should I keep after my child about chores or just do them myself ?

Belonging to a family comes with membership requirements. Each child should be expected to help the parent and to share the housekeeping. The earlier training begins, preferably by age two (cleaning up and picking up and helping out), the less contested chores will be at adolescence when resistance tends to increase, and more pursuit is required to get work done. Do *not* give up and do the child's chores yourself or you will encourage less cooperation, not more. You will cause yourself to feel resentful, burdened by additional work that children should helpfully be doing. *Single parents have enough to do without having to do it all.*

Should I keep after my teenage children to clean up their messy room?

Yes, otherwise, they will use this act of deliberate disorder to justify more serious acts of rebellion and self-rule that are more difficult to curb. They will be encouraged to believe that if they can live in their room any way they want, then they can live the rest of their life on their own terms. They can't. Not yet. So it is worthwhile to make regular clean-up demands and set limits on messiness. By insisting on a minimal degree of upkeep, you specifically and symbolically

167

assert authority in the children's life. Therefore, declare to the children: "I will set minimal standards for order; I won't allow your mess to keep me out; I will knock before I come in; I will inspect at any time; I have the right of search and seizure; and your room will be kept neat and clean enough so I don't feel our home is being trashed." *Single parents need to establish their right to live in surroundings that meet their requirements for order.*

How can I know for sure when my child is ready for more independence?

You can't. Granting independence is always a gamble. With every freedom you allow, the child is placed at further risk. How far can the child play from home? How late can he or she stay out? When to drive? When to date? When to get a job? To gauge the readiness for more independence, assess current evidence of responsibility. When the child demonstrates a capacity for taking care of business at home, at school, and out in the world, only then does the parent agree to risk giving additional freedom of independence. *Single parents want their child to learn more independence as soon as he or she responsibly can.*

My child is always on the telephone. How much is too much?

Too much time is when talking on the phone keeps children up too late, keeps them from getting chores and homework done, keeps them from adequate contact with parents, or keeps the phone tied up so other members of the family have no chance to use it. Otherwise, particularly during adolescence, being on the phone is positive. It keeps teenagers plugged into their social world while remaining under the single parent's supervision. When children are forever talking on the phone, at least they are not out getting into legal trouble, or into car accidents, being sexually active, or becoming hooked on alcohol or drugs. *Single parents need to treat the telephone as an ally that keeps the child connected to friends while he or she remains within the safety of home.*

I wish my children were more responsible with money. As soon as they get it, they spend it. Why can't my children learn to manage money more wisely?

Perhaps because they've never been taught. The best way to instruct is by example. Having told them you want them to keep this information within the family, disclose to the children the specifics of how you manage money. Describe how much money you have to spend each month. Explain to them where it comes from and where it goes. List fixed expenses you must pay, how you budget, and how you decide which bills go first and which can wait until last. Explain how you save what you can, what you are saving for, and when you use credit to obtain now what you must pay for later. Decision making around money is complicated because there is rarely enough for everything one wants. Some gratification needs to be delayed, and some denied. Looking around, there are always other people who are better off. Structure the children's own experience with money. When they earn or are given money, divide it into spending and saving so they can experience and think about the benefits of each. As they grow into adolescence and begin making money, have them pick up some of their own expenses. It feels good to purchase something of value with money one has earned. If the necessity arises, ask them to contribute some of what they earn to support family expenses. This is an important lesson to learn: sometimes it takes multiple salaries to support a single family. Having some earnings for discretionary spending is instructional too. It teaches the time difference between how long it takes to make money and how quickly it can be spent. *Because they have learned how to live on limited resources, single parents are in a very good position to teach their children how to manage money well.*

What should I teach my child about drugs and alcohol?

First, if you choose to drink alcohol, set an example of *moderation* so children can see a model they respect using without compulsion, excess, or harmful effect. Second, if there is any history of drug or alcohol abuse or addiction in the family history, communicate where, and describe what problems have been caused. Explain how this history may elevate the children's risk of having substance problems themselves or getting caught up with others who do. Third, give them the protection of your prohibition: you don't want them using yet. Particularly in mid-adolescence, they may invoke your prohibition as an excuse when saying "no" on their own behalf feels difficult. They can lay the blame on you and the trouble they'll get into should they use. Fourth, because at some age they are likely to experiment, tell them this. "Use is a gamble. Using substances to feel better will put you at risk by altering your mood, your judgment, and perhaps the decisions you would normally make. The best advice I can give, since I cannot make your choices for you, is to *think* before you use. If the pressure is such that you cannot say no, at least play for delay by saying not right now. If you choose to use, don't use more than one substance at a time. Go slowly. Don't show off by getting wasted. Don't drink to get drunk. Don't compete to see who can use or drink the most. Consume in the company of friends you can trust. If you feel compelled to drink, remember that holding a single can of beer for an entire evening can create the appearance of continuous use. If you believe that everyone uses and drinks because all your friends do, then consider expanding your social circle to include friends who neither use nor drink when they have fun together. Don't drive under the influence. Refuse to be driven by others under the influence. If ever you are feeling in danger as a function of your own or someone else's use, call home and I'll come get you. Any time of day or night. No questions asked." *Single parents have to be proactive in discussing alcohol and drugs because the problems of abuse and addiction can be so disabling to a family already coping with so much demand.*

What advice should I give my children about having sex?

Give them a double message. First, you don't want them to have sex yet for a number of important reasons: it can confuse their feelings, hurt their self-image, complicate their relationships, create the responsibility of an unwanted pregnancy, and put them at risk of sexual disease, even death. However, should your child be determined to experience sex as a rite of passage, or to enhance a caring relationship, then give some guidelines, emphasizing the underlined words. "If you are going to have sex, have it sober, with a person you trust, where you do not feel physically or emotionally forced or trapped, where there is enough responsibility or caring to use protection, where you do not feel exploitive or exploited, where you do not assume that sex means love or love forever, where you only do what mutually feels good, where if this relationship ended you would still feel good about yourself for having had sex, and where you do not feel having had sex once you are obliged to have it again." As with substance use, *single parents need to educate their children early about responsible sexual behavior in order to reduce the likelihood of serious problems that can adversely impact the well-being of the entire family.*

171

Now that I am starting to go out again, how will I handle this with the children?

Handle social dating with the same respect that you would expect from them if they were starting to go out. Give the children adequate information. Tell them where you are going, with whom, how you can be reached, and when you will return. Promise that if there is any change in plans, you will call and let them know. If the children are very young or you have not gone out since the death or divorce, understand that your leaving is an act of separation. This temporary absence may take some getting used to by the children. Initially, they may need assurances before you go and a call while you are away. In addition, they must feel comfortable and secure with whomever is charged with their care while you are gone. *Single parents need a separate social life from children who need to feel safe when they are left behind.*

How can I decide if I should get serious about a romantic relationship?

Ask yourself three questions. First, do I like how I treat myself in this relationship? For example, do I speak up about my wants and feelings when I don't like what's happening to me? Second, do I like how I treat the other person in the relationship? For example, can I listen when we disagree without automatically criticizing or correcting the other person's point of view? Third, do I like how the other person treats me in the relationship? For example, when we fight does he or she express frustration and anger in a manner I do not find threatening or demeaning? Unless you can answer all three questions with an unqualified "yes," the relationship does not yet justify your commitment. *Single parents need to proceed with reasonable caution before committing to a new relationship, allowing their head to have the final say over their heart.*

Suppose I decide to remarry. Can I expect the children and my new partner to get along as well together after marriage as they did before?

No. Role changes (from romantic lover to committed spouse) change relationships. When you all move into one home, separation is lost and the honeymoon is over. The period of courtship when everyone was on best behavior, when good times were the only times everyone had, is past. Now more bad times must be managed, and there will be moments when other people are revealed at their worst. Everyone must now share space and resources together. Everyone must make room for each other. Everyone must daily coexist around some differences that will be hard to tolerate. Everyone will occasionally find themselves in conflict over competing wants. Everyone will encounter disagreements about rules and responsibilities. The adults will have to struggle with defining just how much parenting the stepparent is prepared to do, and the children will have to struggle with how much compliance they are prepared to give to this person who is not really their parent. Expect more family tension and complexity, and commit to remarriage across three levels of intimacy. Commit on a *personal* level to get to know each other as individuals. Commit on a *partnering* level to share common decisions that enhance your sense of mutuality. And commit on a *parental* level to construct and conduct a family together. Never treat issues with the children in a way that becomes divisive of the marriage. Rather, approach these inevitable problems with the children as part of the challenge of remarriage. Understand that by talking them through, you each will get to know the other in ways you otherwise could not. *Single parents and their new spouse need to commit to a remarriage that is complicated by step differences, resolved to treat those differences not as a source of divisiveness, but as a source of richness that can deepen the intimacy between them.*

GLOSSARY

Adolescence The period between when a young person leaves childhood, around the age of puberty, and finally grows up enough to accept young adult responsibilities eight to ten years later.

Burnout A state of apathy induced by protracted stress, causing people to lose caring about what happens to themselves, about what happens to others, and about life in general.

Child support A monthly contribution of payments that the noncustodial parent, as a function of a divorce decree or established paternity, agrees to pay the custodial parent to help support their child.

Compensation The act of making up to oneself or others in the present for some perceived deficiency in the past.

Consent A child's willingness to go along with what a parent wants and does not want to have happen.

Custody The legal guardianship of the child. As part of divorce, one parent is either granted custody, the other parent becoming the noncustodial parent, or custody may be shared, as in joint custody.

Deprivation A form of punishment through which parents reduce a child's freedom or take away a privilege as a consequence of some major wrongdoing.

Developmental lumphood That phase of early adolescence when a child seems to lack energy for doing anything except lying around and complaining about being bored.

Divorce The legal dissolution of a marriage.

Emotional extortion A tactic of manipulation in which the intense expression of emotionality is used to overcome resistance from the other person in order to get one's way.

Emotional protest The expression of fear, frustration, anger, hurt, or helplessness in response to an unwanted change in life.

Exchange points When asked by the child to provide some permission, service, or resources, parents withhold what is wanted until the child has done what they requested first, thereby invoking the principle of exchange in the relationship. One has to give in order to receive.

Garnish wages Collecting child support from a delinquent ex-partner by legally forcing required payments to be deducted from that person's salary.

Mentor An interested person from whose greater experience and knowledge one can learn.

Moderation Practicing a pattern of performance and consumption that does not resort to extremes to satisfy feelings for enough.

Mourning The process of healing hurt from significant losses (like death or divorce) through active grieving, by letting in, letting out, and finally letting go of the pain.

Mutuality Living in a relationship in such a way that attention to the needs of oneself and others are balanced.

Nagging An act of supervision whereby, through repetitive asking, parents wear down the child's resistance to doing what he or she does not want to do.

Need to be known The individual being willing to express sufficient self-definition in relationships so others are kept adequately informed about what that person feels, thinks, wants, and believes.

Need to know The individual keeping adequately informed about other people in the family so that anxiety from ignorance about what is happening in their lives is at a minimum.

Reparation A form of punishment through which parents assign a task that would not ordinarily have to be done as a consequence for wrongdoing, with the child required to pay for the misdeed by working it off.

Resistance Opposing unwanted demands from others or opposing adjustments to unwanted changes in life.

Self-maintenance Acting to take care of one's minimal needs for well-being on a daily basis.

Social cruelty The period roughly coinciding with grades three to six, when children act to protect their early adolescent insecurities by attacking each other's vulnerabilities in order to establish social standing or achieve popularity.

Social embarrassment That period of early adolescence when children no longer want to be seen publicly by peers in the company of their parents.

Social extortion A common means of applying pressure used by mid-adolescent children who ask for parental permission in front of a group of waiting friends in order to make it more difficult for the mother or father to ask questions or to say "no."

Trial independence The last stage of adolescence (roughly between ages eighteen and twenty-three) when the young person is struggling for the first time to live on his or her own.

Visitation The scheduled contact between children and their noncustodial parent after divorce.

SUGGESTED READING

Alexander, Shoshana. *In Praise of Single Parents*. New York: Houghton Mifflin, 1994.

Bailey, Marilyn. *Single-parent Families*. New York: Crestwood House, 1989.

Berman, Eleanor. *The Cooperating Family*. Englewood Cliffs, New Jersey: Prentice-Hall, 1977.

Fontenelle, Don H. *Keys to Parenting Your Teenager*. Hauppauge, New York: Barron's Educational Series, Inc., 1992.

Gardner, Richard A. *The Boys and Girls Book about One-Parent Families*. New York: Putnam, 1978.

Pickhardt, C. E. *Parenting The Teenager*. P.O. Box 50022, Austin, Texas, 78763, 1983.

Polakow, Valerie. *Lives on the Edge*. Chicago: The University of Chicago Press, 1993.

The Single Parent Magazine. 8807 Colesville Road, Silver Spring, Maryland, 20910.

SUPPORT GROUPS

We live in an age of self-help groups that can be truly helpful. Most do not charge for their services or are sustained by voluntary contributions from members. These groups provide fellowship for people sharing common problems. They provide useful information and valuable support.

The diversity of the groups available depends largely on the size of the community in which you live. A large city would have the most variety, a small town the least. To find out what groups are available in your area, call the local or state mental health association, or inquire through local schools, hospitals, or churches. To make contact with a particular group, consult your local phone directory.

A few groups you may find helpful include:

The National Organization of Single Parents (support resources, referrals, benefits. P.O. Box 41522, Washington, D.C. 20018)

Parents Without Partners (focusing on fellowship and support for single parents)

Parents Anonymous (providing a gathering place where parenting issues of all kinds can be helpfully discussed)

Tough Love (providing support and a structured program for those parents whose children are breaking significant rules and are refusing to abide parental control)

Al-Anon (providing help living around a loved one's problem use of chemicals)

INDEX

179

Rituals, 23
Role models, 83–85
Routines, 23

School performance, 108–110
Self-centeredness, 97–100
Self-definition, 73–74
Self-maintenance, 39–42
Self-sufficiency, 60–63
Sensitivity, 71
Separation, 75
Sex, 171
Sex role models, 83–85
Sharing, 75
Sharing child care, 44
Sibling conflict, 80–82
Social cruelty, 114–116
Social extortion, 98
Socialization, 74

Social support, 43–45
Speaking up, 52–53
Speed (in parent's life), 33
Standards, 33–34, 74–75
Stress, 35–38
Structure, 56–57
Supervision, 56
Support groups, 178

Taking charge, 28–31
Teenagers. *See* Adolescents
Telephone, 168–169
Television, 86–88
Transition, 1–4
Trial independence, 105–107

Visitation, 135–138

Widowhood, loneliness of, 149–152